Clipper Ships

A clipper was any vessel designed to sail as fast as possible and to carry cargo. Clippers could be of any size and of any rig. Clippers were at their peak in the years 1845–1875. Only a handful of clippers were ever built, compared with the mass of cargo-carrying ships sailing the seas.

Clipper ships have always captured the imagination of artists, and here Charles Robert Patterson depicts the Flying Cloud in a freshening breeze with the wind abeam, some of her crew aloft, furling the fore royal. This ship built in 1851 by Donald McKay and was of 1782 tons. (San Francisco Maritime Museum).

Clipper
Ships

David R. MacGregor

Model and Allied Publications
Published by Argus Books Ltd, 14 St James Road,
Watford, Herts, England

© Argus Books Ltd 1979
© David R. MacGregor, 1979

ISBN 0 85242 618 6

First published 1979

Dedicated
To Julia and Charles Sumner Bird

By the same Author:

The Tea Clippers
(1952, reprinted 1972)
The China Bird (1961)
Fast Sailing Ships 1775–1875 (1973)
Square Rigged Sailing Ships (1977)

Contents

Introduction

Each time I start to write about clipper ships, I think I shall have to repeat myself and rehearse the same facts, tell the same stories, use the same illustrations, but it is surprising how new material comes to hand and that in thinking again on how to rephrase well-known events, a different angle presents itself. Instead of being a challenge difficult to surmount, the work now assumes quite a new outlook and one can view the subject with a degree of maturity.

In the present case, I have tried to present an equal amount on American clippers to compare with their British counterparts, but in attempting to present an unbiased view of the matter, I find I am inevitably taking sides. The causes behind clipper design in the two countries produced such differing results that it seems only sensible to divide the clippers of the respective countries into separate chapters. Unfortunately, I have not collected a great deal about clippers built on the Continent of Europe, but then few clippers were built there compared with Britain and America.

The selection of the pictures is always a soul-jerking task, but when the final count is made, I wonder what all the fuss was about. Karl Kortum, Director of the San Francisco Maritime Museum, suggested that I use actual photographs of clippers rather than photographs of prints or paintings, and this has been the general theme. More high quality photographs of American clippers of the fifties seem available than for British ships of the same decade, either because there were keener American ship photographers in the last century, or else because there were keener collectors in this. Karl Kortum and his staff have given great help in advising on sources and providing many of the pictures.

Over many years, I could always count on the accurate advice and information supplied by John Lyman, but his untimely death at the end of 1977 has robbed, not only myself, but all his friends and ship researchers throughout the world, of a person who it will be difficult, perhaps impossible, to replace.

Continuing with others who have provided illustrations in America, I am grateful to Andrew Nesdall for several rare photographs; to Robert Weinstein, for advice on sources; to John Shedd of Model Shipways for permission to reproduce plans of *Flying Fish*; and to Richard Parker.

I take pleasure in acknowledging the generous assistance given at various maritime

[**Opposite**] *Sitting bolt upright in the Albert Graving Dock at Williamstown, Victoria, the* Salamis *is in an ideal position to observe her long fine entrance and perfect lines. Intended for the tea trade, she was built much too late.* (The late D. M. Little).

1

museums such as the Peabody Museum, Mystic Seaport, and the Mariners Museum, and in particular I should like to thank John Lockhead of the latter for providing copies of plans in the Hillmann and Guibert Collections.

In Australia, Roderick Glassford and Cyril Hume have sent me many rare photographs from their collections; so also did the late David M. Little and Arthur D. Edwardes. I have corresponded and exchanged pictures with all four of them over many years.

In Britain, I should like to record my thanks to the staff of the Print Room at the National Maritime Museum and in particular to George A. Osbon; likewise to Basil Bathe, late Curator of Shipping at the Science Museum; to Michael Stammers of the Liverpool Museum; and to A. S. E. Browning of the Glasgow Museum and Art Galleries. Amongst shipbuilders whose plans and records I have examined, I am grateful to Alexander Stephen & Sons Ltd and to their chief draughtsman, R. W. McGregor; to Barclay, Curle & Co; and to John C. G. Hill of Charles Hill & Son.

Of private collectors, my especial thanks go to my old friend James Henderson who most generously drew a sail plan of *Cairngorm* at short notice and provided several photographs. I should like to acknowledge the help given by Bertram Newbury of the Parker Gallery for permission to look through their files and reproduce various pictures. I am grateful to a number of friends who have provided either illustrations or information, perhaps both, including Gustav Alexanderson, G. Matsen, Heinrich Walle and Roger Finch.

For permission to use the drawing of *Cutty Sark*, I should like to thank Vice-Admiral Sir Patrick Bayly, Director of the *Cutty Sark* Society. For preparing and executing several plans under my direction, I am grateful to Paul Roberts for his excellent draughtsmanship; to George Weston for all the old photographs he has copied; and to Ken Peeling of Pisces Litho for copying the plans.

David R. MacGregor   Barnes, London, 1979

CHAPTER ONE

Hull Analysis and Classification

In the past it has been generally accepted that any ship or craft that could sail fast deserved the title of 'clipper' and scant regard was given to the shape of her hull or the means by which she achieved her speed. Most ships built during the 1850s and 1860s were thought to be clippers, and it was anathema to suggest that any ship venturing out to China, Australia or the Californian gold fields was anything else. But it is time that such romantic nonsense was terminated once and for all, and so before describing the clippers themselves it would be a good idea if the terms for such descriptions were themselves fully explored and also if the clipper characteristics were analyzed and the various types of vessels classified.

It is important to realize that a clipper could be of any size and rig. In size from, say, 50 tons and upwards. In rig, they could be full-rigged ships, barques, brigs, brigantines, jackass barques, or schooners. Curiously enough, cutters are not usually included although, as will be later shown, they usually possessed a clipper's characteristics. This also applies to luggers and chebecs. But just as the size and rig varied, so could the 'hull-form', that is to say, the shape and form of the hull as given her by the shipbuilder or naval architect, so that there were endless permutations.

A clipper was designed for a particular trade and to carry a specialized cargo, often accompanied by passengers, but always with the aim of achieving maximum speed. The cargo was frequently perishable or valuable and the ships which carried it could command high rates of freight. Above average remuneration was necessary to foster and maintain clippers, because the achievement of speed required the hulls to be as fine below the water as yachts, which inevitably reduced the cargo capacity.

The following characteristics should be present to enable a vessel to qualify as a 'clipper':

(1) A fine-lined hull.
(2) An emphasis on streamlined appearance.
(3) A large sail area.
(4) A daring and skilful master.

But it was no good just qualifying as a clipper; to obtain the speed and short passages for which she was designed, a ship had to have a capable and daring master. This fourth point was as important as the other three. Here we have a conundrum that a daring and skilful master could sometimes make a fast passage with a full-bodied ship, whereas a timorous and inept master could never make a fast passage with the finest-lined clipper that was ever built.

Before considering the above points in greater detail, some definitions of the terms employed may not be out of place.

As the 'lines' comprise the outlines of the hull, the contours of which are delineated in the horizontal, vertical and oblique sections, so 'fine-lined' or 'sharp-lined' imply a hull-form that is the opposite of bluff or full-bodied. Fineness of hull-form can also be deduced by viewing an actual hull out of the water although it is principally the shape of the waterlines that can most easily be judged. The 'entrance' is the shape of the fore part of the hull; the 'run' is the after part of the hull, and these two parts are jointly called the 'ends'. The 'midship section' or 'mid-section' is that part of the ship where the hull is at its broadest, and it is generally equi-distant between bow and stern, although in some clippers the broadest part did not coincide with the midship section. 'Deadrise' or 'rise of floor' is the angle of the bottom planking between keel and bilge compared with a base line at right angles to the keel; if the angle is small, the ship is said to have 'flat' floors or 'little deadrise'; if the angle is large, then the deadrise is described as 'steep' or 'sharp'. It is hoped that the reader has some knowledge on how to read the waterlines, sections and buttock lines which are the contours on the sheer elevation, half-breadth plan and body plan, and which together form the 'lines plan'. In any case, the plan of the clipper *Stornoway* on page 7 has them marked on.

Let us now consider the clipper characteristics in greater detail.

Firstly, a fine-lined hull required an underwater body with a sharp entrance and run in which there were no bumps or sudden curves to spoil the even sweep of the lines. In some cases there was very steep deadrise in addition to extremely sharp ends, but often there was a compromise between deadrise and fineness at bow and stern. Consideration had to be given to the type of weather likely to be encountered and the cargo to be carried. Thus clippers bound for the Californian gold fields that had to beat round Cape Horn or run before the westerly winds to Australia, often had less deadrise than those intended to bring back tea from China or fruit from the Azores. But then again, designers differed in their opinions. While some preferred a marked hollow in the waterlines at the entrance, others insisted that they be convex; while William Pile and others employed a shorter entrance but a longer run, the protagonists of the 'wave line theory' needed the opposite with a long entrance and a short run. Nevertheless, whatever variations were employed the result was a vessel whose lines were designed for speed and for making fast passages.

When studying the lines plan, the sharpness of the entrance at the load waterline quickly indicates the vessel's speed potential. Another point to look for is the shape of the buttock line in the run, when spaced at a quarter of the vessel's maximum beam; this is termed the 'quarter beam buttock' and for a fast hull this line should be almost straight from above the load line to some distance below. A long hull has greater potential for speed than a short one, and the proportion of beams to length is sometimes judged of importance. Iron hulls could be more easily built long and narrow than in the case of wooden ones and some very unusual designs were produced in Scotland in the 1850s.

The second clipper characteristic was defined as having a streamlined appearance, by which is meant that the heavy headwork, massive stern galleries and uneven sheer line were superseded. Storm goddesses with outstretched arms, nymphs with golden tresses, eagles that could brave the elements or warriors that could command the winds were placed under the bowsprit where the raking stem and an unbroken sheer line met. Such figureheads were supported by elegant trail boards in most British ships,

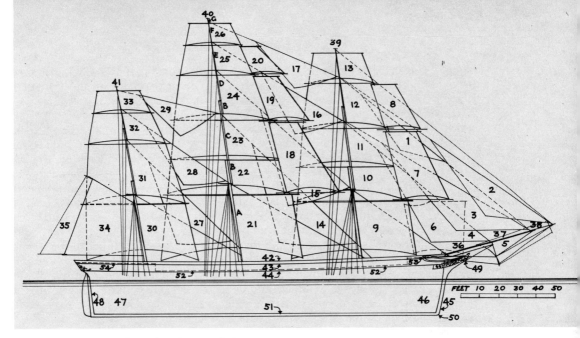

Diagrammatic sail plan of a clipper of the sixties.

KEY

1	Jib topsail	17	Main skysail staysail	32	Mizen topgallant sail	47	Run
2	Flying jib	18	Main topmast stunsail	33	Mizen royal	48	Stern post
3	Jib	19	Main topgallant stunsail	34	Spanker	49	Figurehead
4	Fore topmast staysail	20	Main royal stunsail	35	Ringtail	50	Fore foot
5	Jamie Green	21	Mainsail (or Main course)	36	Bowsprit	51	Keel
6	Fore lower stunsail	22	Main lower topsail	37	Jibboom	52	Deck level
7	Fore topmast stunsail	23	Main upper topsail	38	Flying jibboom	53	Monkey foc'sle
8	Fore topgallant stunsail	24	Main topgallant sail	39	Fore mast	54	Raised quarter-deck
9	Foresail (or Fore course)	25	Main royal	40	Main mast	A	Lower mast
10	Fore lower topsail	26	Main skysail	41	Mizen mast	B	Doubling
11	Fore upper topsail	27	Mizen topmast staysail	42	Topgallant rail	C	Topmast
12	Fore topgallant sail	28	Mizen topgallant staysail	43	Main rail	D	Topgallant mast
13	Fore royal	29	Mizen royal staysail	44	Plancksheer	E	Royal mast
14	Main topmast staysail	30	Crossjack	45	Stem	F	Skysail mast
15	Main topgallant staysail	31	Mizen topsail	46	Entrance	G	Mast head
16	Main royal staysail						

although in America the bow was often bare and devoid of almost any decoration except for the figurehead. Perhaps one is allowed some romantic nostalgia in the way the bows were adorned. The desire of achieving an unbroken sheer line was undoubtedly carried to absurd lengths in some cases which resulted in inconvenient accommodation arrangements in poop or forecastle. For instance, in the Aberdeen clipper *Black Prince* of 1863, the naval architect William Rennie made the headroom inside the forecastle only five feet at the after end, so that men had to bend double to get through the doorway on to the deck. Aft, the placing of the accommodation in a house abaft the mizen which was surrounded by a low deck below the top of the rail was one way of achieving an unbroken sheer at the stern. This 'Aberdeen house' can be seen in the *Cutty Sark* today. Iron ships achieved the object by curving down the ends of the deck beams on to the rail surrounding the poop. This was called a 'half-round'. With the hull painted black, and the half-round painted white, the result was that the accommodation did not obtrude on the lovely sheer.

Meanwhile, as rigging techniques improved and wire standing rigging replaced hemp rigging in British ships in the 1850s, the cumbersome channels which projected from a ship's side were no longer required. By contrast, American and Canadian clippers continued to use not only one but two channels to set up the rigging.

The third clipper characteristic was a large sail area. In addition to the 'plain' sails which are those set from the yards and stays, studding sails could also be set from booms which were extended outside the yards on the fore and main masts, and it was normal for the studding sails or 'stunsails', as the word has been corrupted, to each equal half the area of the sail or sails outside of which they were set. Thus the area of plain canvas could be doubled on a mast if stunsails were set each side. Stunsails were regular sails on every vessel up to the end of the 1860s, whether the ship was a clipper or a carrier, although the fancy sails carried by clippers such as stunsails that could be set beside the skysails, moonsails that could be set above skysails, ringtails that were hauled out abaft the spanker, watersails that were rigged below the lower stunsails, and Jamie Greens that appeared under the jibbooms were all referred to as 'flying kites'. If the usual sail area needed on a full-ended ship was placed on a clipper, the result was that an average speed was obtained. But clippers went one better by increasing the normal sail area, sometimes to an alarming degree, so that the safety factor was open to question unless the ship was most expertly handled.

Fourthly, the master's degree of verve in driving his ship continuously day and night under all conditions of wind and weather required the highest stamina and skill possible, and was manifested in all too few men. Not least was the ability of knowing where to find fair winds, and until the findings were published by such people as Maury, it was often a closely-guarded secret. 'Passage-making' was quite an art.

There are numerous log-book extracts to indicate the manner in which the large sail areas were employed to drive the ships along; and to set too many sails in heavy weather or not to furl them in a rising wind was known as 'carrying on'. On the maiden passage of the American extreme clipper *Lightning* across the Atlantic in 1854, the entry for 1st March reads in part: 'Hove the log several times and found the ship going through the water at the rate of 18 to $18\frac{1}{2}$ knots, lee rail under water and rigging slack'. For a ship with a freeboard of 12 to 15 feet this shows how hard she was being driven. In the same ship on her first passage from Liverpool to Melbourne under the command of Captain Forbes, a passenger wrote in his diary for 7th July 1854:

'10pm. Top gallant sails not taken in although the blocks 18 inches above the lee rail are frequently under water—the deck is on an angle of 45° to 50° . . . The second mate, whose watch it is, says "Now this is what I call carrying on".'

It will be noticed that the *Lightning* has just been defined as an 'extreme' clipper. There are three categories into which clippers fall: extreme clippers, clippers, and medium clippers. 'Extreme clippers' were built on excessively fine lines with hulls more like large yachts and with little thought of cargo capacity; a return on their investment rested entirely with their ability to achieve unusually fast passages at a time when freight rates were at a peak. 'Clippers' were not so extreme yet they possessed very fine-lined hulls, and usually achieved passages quite as fast as the 'extreme' clippers; they could earn a better living when freight rates fell. The majority of clippers fall into the second category. 'Medium clippers' on the other hand were really sharpened versions of a cargo carrier, but with a good master and favourable winds they might make a passage as fast or faster than the extreme clipper. Examples of all three will be given here, although emphasis will be on the first two categories.

For the most accurate manner of comparing the intrinsic capabilities and poten-

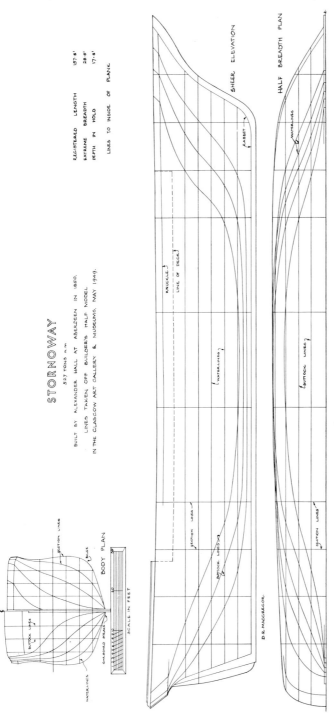

STORNOWAY

527 TONS n.m

BUILT BY ALEXANDER HALL AT ABERDEEN IN 1850.

LINES TAKEN OFF BUILDER'S HALF MODEL
IN THE GLASGOW ART GALLERY & MUSEUMS, MAY 1949.

REGISTERED LENGTH   157' 8'
EXTREME BREADTH   28' 8'
DEPTH IN HOLD   17' 8'

LINES TO INSIDE OF PLANK.

SHEER ELEVATION

HALF BREADTH PLAN

BODY PLAN

SCALE IN FEET

D.R. MACGREGOR.

This drawing is a 'lines plan' of the clipper ship Stornoway and some of the principal parts are described. This ship was built at Aberdeen in 1850 for the China tea trade. (Author).

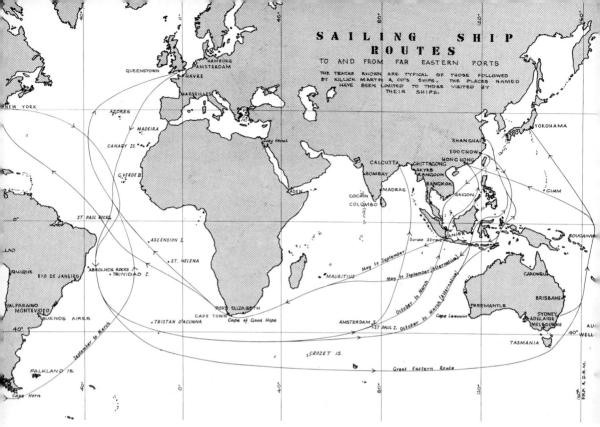

SAILING SHIP
ROUTES
TO AND FROM FAR EASTERN PORTS

THE TRACKS SHOWN ARE TYPICAL OF THOSE FOLLOWED
BY KILLICK MARTIN & CO'S SHIPS. THE PLACES NAMED
HAVE BEEN LIMITED TO THOSE VISITED BY
THEIR SHIPS.

tialities of clippers, the displacement needs to be calculated, but this requires a more detailed study than is possible here. The Prismatic Coefficient employs the area of the midship section below the load line; the Block Coefficient is the ratio of the displacement to the product of the length, breadth and depth.

A crude approximation is to substitute under-deck tonnage for displacement, and in my first book, *The Tea Clippers*, I described it more fully and provided a list of coefficients for twenty-five tea clippers. Fine-lined ships usually had a ratio of .60 or less. For anyone wishing to try this last method for himself, it should be noted that one ton equals 100 cubic feet; so that after multiplying the under-deck tonnage by 100, it should be divided by the product of the register dimensions. I refer to this as the 'Coefficient of Under-Deck Tonnage'. Of course, under-deck tonnage does not appear prior to the Merchant Shipping Act of 1854.

Another ratio that can be deduced without the displacement is the 'speed–length ratio', which is obtained by dividing the highest speed a ship is known to have attained (in knots) by the square root of the load line length (in feet). Any ship whose ratio exceeds 1.25 is a fast vessel.

A rule of thumb method is the comparison of 'old' and 'new' measurement tonnage figures, which can be employed for vessels built between 1836 and 1854. It has been shown that a considerably smaller new measurement tonnage figure indicates sharp hull-form. A comparison between two of Alexander Hall's ships, for which half-models exist, gives the following figures:

Benjamin Elkin   built 1849; 367 new and 425 old tons = fine lined.
Alexander Hall   built 1845; 403 new and 358 old tons = full-bodied.

[**Above**] *This model of the* James Baines *illustrates an American clipper of the largest size. She was built in 1854 by Donald McKay. The model shows her hollow entrance lines and her high sides. When she first reached Liverpool, skysail yards were added to fore and main masts, and a moonsail above the main skysail.* (Parker Gallery).

[**Opposite**] *Although this chart only covers trade routes between Europe, Eastern America and the Far East, it demonstrates the courses which sailing ships were obliged to follow in their search for favourable winds.* (Author).

What a seeming anachronism that Alexander Hall—that inventor of the raking Aberdeen bow and designer of some of the most celebrated clippers—should have had a full-bodied barque named after him. But the ship named after Donald McKay was a medium clipper with a flat bottom and large cargo capacity.

In *Fast Sailing Ships: their Design and Construction, 1775–1875*, I limited the definition of 'clipper' only to vessels whose plans or half-models I had examined, thereby narrowing the field to a proven *élite*. Here a wider spectrum is presented which comprises both the authentic clipper as well as those for which no plans or models are known to exist but which are judged to be clippers because of fast passages, reliable contemporary definitions, or illustrations. I do not wish to labour the point, but speed and looks do not qualify a ship for a clipper status, although they can support her as a candidate. So there are a number of quasi-clippers pictured here which have always raced or been pictured with the proven *élite*. The clippers of the front rank were often called 'full bloods' or 'cracks' and indeed much terminology of the turf was applied to clipper ship races.

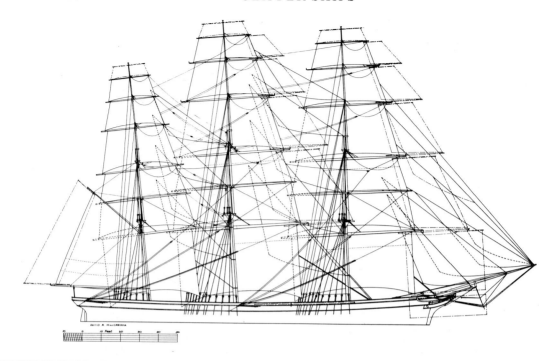

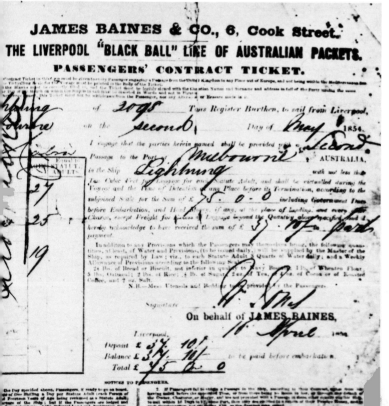

[**Above**] *This sail plan of the British clipper* Maitland *depicts an amazing cloud of canvas with skysails and moonsails on each mast, apart from numerous flying kites. She was built at Sunderland in 1865 of 799 tons. Plan drawn by David R. MacGregor. (Author).*

[**Left**] *Passenger's Contract Ticket aboard the* Lightning *on her maiden passage from Liverpool to Melbourne in 1854 under the Command of Captain J. N. Forbes. Passage money was £75. (M. Costagliola).*

A drawing of the Cutty Sark under full sail, with the starboard side cut away to show the stowage of tea chests, position of masts, layout of 'tween deck etc. (Cutty Sark Society).

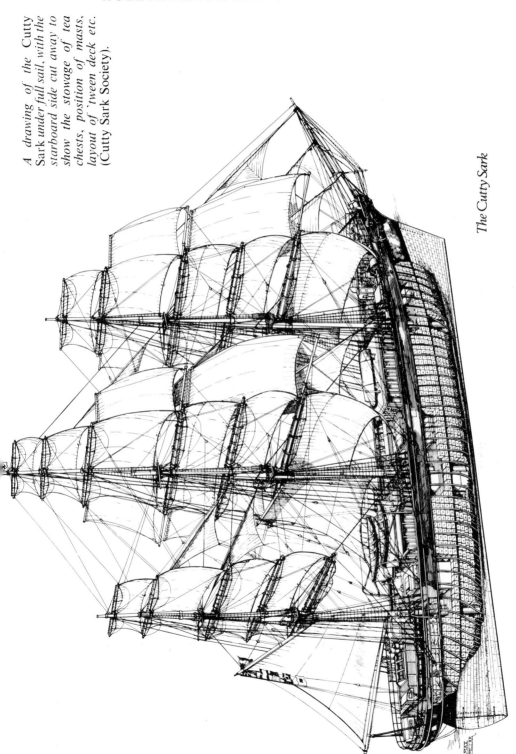

The Cutty Sark

CHAPTER TWO

Fast Ships before 1830

The clipper ship boom began almost simultaneously in Britain and America, being sparked off by the discovery of gold in California in 1849, the Repeal of the British Navigation Laws in the same year, and the finding of gold in Australia in 1851. The urgent need for fast ships to fulfil the demands of gold-hungry passengers did not fall on a shipbuilding market destitute of ideas as fine-lined vessels had been constructed fairly regularly over the previous century in both countries, although it was in wartime that the majority were launched. Apart from ships to be fitted out as privateers during the American War of Independence, the Napoleonic Wars in Europe and the Naval War of 1812, there was always a need for fast ships to carry fruit, opium, perishable goods, tea, passengers and the mail. Slavers, smugglers, revenue cutters and yachts also required to be fast.

In Great Britain an indigenous type of craft built for speed was the cutter. These had broad hulls in which the length was usually between $2\frac{1}{2}$ to 3 times the breadth; but they had great deadrise with steep floors and fine but convex waterlines. In addition they had a great spread of canvas and regularly crossed two, three or even four yards, so that both fore-and-aft and square sails could be set. Many cutters were in the 50 to 150 tons range and the largest were of about 250 tons. By the end of the eighteenth century, schooners and brigs were being built with cutter hulls so that the term 'cutter-built' implied the same as 'clipper-built' did later. A 'cutter-brig' was another term used to denote a brig built with a cutter's hull-form.

In a sketchbook by Thomas Luny at the National Maritime Museum are drawings and notes he made in 1779 of the cutter *Hector,* of prodigious size owned by a Mr Smith. Overall length on deck was 95 ft from stem to taffrail; maximum breadth on deck was 29 ft 6 in; draft of water aft was 14 ft, forward was 7 ft. No tonnage is given. Based on a hull profile he drew and other sketches he made, a spar and sail plan can be drawn to utilize the spar dimensions Luny listed. The spars were of fantastic dimensions; the mainmast was 102 ft long overall with a maximum diameter of 29 ins; the main boom was 74 ft 6 ins; the bowsprit was 70 ft and the jibboom was 62 ft. Four yards are specified as well as a boom for the foot of the square sail. As was customary in large cutters, a mizen was also provided, to be stepped right aft, and given a pronounced rake. It was 44 ft long and on it a lugsail was set from a 40 ft yard, the sheet being hauled out to an outrigger 44 ft long overall. The stepping of the mast and outrigger would have been similar to that adopted for the mizen in the lugger illustrated on page 15. The *Hector's* occupation or trade is unknown but one suspects it may not have been legal.

In Great Britain, an Act of 1784 proscribed cutters, luggers, shallops, wherries, smacks or yawls unless they were 'square-rigged', and this may be one reason why cutters were given so much square canvas, although licences could be obtained for vessels in legitimate trade. This Act was a crude attempt to curtail smuggling. It also prohibited a beam-to-length ratio greater than $3\frac{1}{2}$ to 1, a prohibition that was still in

A large and heavily-rigged cutter drawn by Edward Gwyn in about 1780. This looks as if it was drawn to scale and everything is in proportion, although the four yards seem rather short. The deeply roached foot of the topsail was typical, although here it is excessive. Between the gunports are ports for oars to row her in a calm. A stern elevation is on the right. (National Maritime Museum).

force in 1833, but when it was dropped is uncertain. This regulation must have been partly responsible for the broad beam and short length retained by cutters.

Cutters were employed in various legitimate ways: in carrying mail and passengers from Great Britain to Ireland and the Continent, or along the coast; the fruit trade had some cutters; in time of war they could obtain letters of marque; yachts and pilot boats were cutters. The Leith smacks, which were cutters, were more full-bodied than one would have expected, but they could occasionally cover the route of 460 miles between Leith and London in about 50 hours. During the 1830s, many of the large cutters were being lengthened and rerigged as schooners.

Luggers had much the same hull as a cutter but often they were longer vessels, and the French lugger *Le Coureur* of 1775 is a good example. Her plan (opposite) shows a craft with big deadrise and fine lines; her bulwarks have four gun ports cut in her side; she is rigged with three masts and topsails on each, and there is a long bowsprit. This rig and hull-form persisted in both France and England as well as other European countries until the middle of the nineteenth century. In wartime they were ideal as privateers; in peacetime they were equally suitable as smugglers, and some very long craft were constructed.

In America, luggers do not appear to have been in use commercially, but sloops on the Bermudian model as well as a few cutters were employed prior to the War of Independence. But the schooner early gained prominence on the New England coast and became one of the most popular rigs after about 1770. Many of these schooners, as well as brigs and ships, were captured by the Royal Navy and plans which were prepared of them are now among the Admiralty Draughts at the National Maritime Museum. By this means, the hull-form can be studied and the sail plans reconstructed from the spar dimensions given.

Although the cutters had steep deadrise, their short length and great beam required the waterlines to fill out quickly; they also required a deep hull to balance the large sail area. The American schooners and brigs repeated the steep floors but the longer and narrower hulls enabled finer waterlines in entrance and run, and also avoided the deep draft of the cutter. Prior to 1793, most of the schooners were less than 80 ft in length.

During the French Revolution, Chesapeake Bay shipyards, of which Baltimore was the chief, gained a reputation for building fast-sailing brigs and schooners, so much so that in 1798 the French Government agents secretly purchased a number of fast vessels there, as well as at other ports. Thus was developed the reputation of the 'Baltimore clipper' on both sides of the Atlantic.

Owing to the influence which pilot boats had on fast-sailing design, the term 'pilot-boat model' is often to be found as describing a vessel built for speed. The late Howard Chapelle studied all these craft in detail and redrew many of the old plans for reproduction in his various books. Some of the large schooners, such as the *Nonpereil* (built 1807 of 191 tons) had a great drag aft and this feature was carried to excess in the schooner *Grecian* of 1812. Many of the vessels built during the Naval War of 1812 were longer than formerly and they also carried more square canvas, sometimes crossing two or three yards on the topmasts of both masts. One of the best known was the brigantine *Prince de Neuchâtel*, built at New York in 1812–13 of 328 tons, and mounting sixteen 12-pounder carronades; her design was the basis for the opium clipper *Red Rover* which was famous for her speed.

The steep-floored American brigs and schooners were much admired in Europe, particularly in France, where many fast privateers were built during the Napoleonic

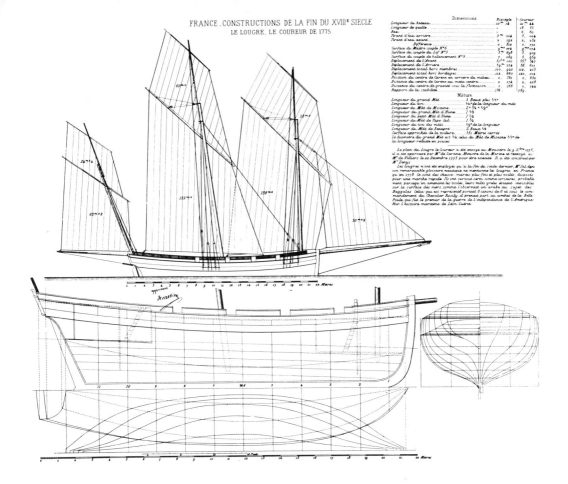

Sail plan and Lines plan of the three-masted French lugger Le Coureur *of 1775, as drawn for* Souvenirs de Marine *by Admiral Paris. She carried 8 guns and was built to sail fast. There was only the minimum of rigging to support the sturdy masts. Length is given as 21.44 m × 6.60 m × 3.00 m draft at stern. (Author).*

wars to harass British shipping. Amongst the Guibert Collection of plans at the Mariners' Museum, Newport News, are several vessels with very steep floors and fine waterlines, such as the three-masted *L'Intrepide* designed for Citizen Elizé Nairac. She has eleven gunports, a plain stem with only a gammon knee, three masts, a flush deck, maximum beam at the load line, with very steep floors and waterlines that are fine and convex. The brig *Phoenix* of 1808 is of similar design, except that she has the traditional knees and headrails to support a conventional figurehead. The straight steep floors to be seen in such designs was at variance with the traditional French bodyplan which more resembled the shape of a pear, and which can be found in the plans of the four-masted ship *L'Invention*. This remarkable vessel was constructed in 1800–01 with a very raking stem and a long hull with extremely fine lines, but her claim to fame is that she had four masts with square sails on each, thus making her the first four-masted full-rigged ship. Her dimensions were 135 ft 5 ins length on lower deck, 27 ft 5 ins extreme breadth and about 14 ft 6 ins depth of hold; tonnage was given as 486 tons. From a painting done of her in Naples in 1803, Basil Lubbock wrote that on her jigger mast she carried nothing above a topgallant, but on fore, main and mizen masts she set royals.* She was captured by the British frigate *Immortalité* when the privateer was on her first cruise. No spar dimensions are listed on her plan.

In Great Britain, fast-sailing privateers on the Baltimore model were built less frequently and examples of full-rigged ships and brigs that are reproduced in my book, *Fast Sailing Ships: their Design and Construction, 1775–1875*, show a variety of designs. The *Shamrock* was a Revenue brig, built in 1805 as the *Resolution*, with the hull-form of a cutter. A queer vessel was the *Transit*, built in 1800 as a barquentine, first with five and later with four masts; she had fine lines and a long narrow hull. An even longer barquentine of the same name replaced her in 1809 having 5.9 beams to length. Referring to yet a third *Transit*, launched in 1819, a waterman who boarded her in the Thames called her a 'clipper'.

The British Post Office packets needed to be fast, especially as the authorities decided that they should be lightly armed to deter them from taking prizes, and they therefore were obliged to trust to speed as a means of escape if pursued. The official size was given as 179 tons, and a plan in the Hilhouse Collection of an unnamed packet shows the influence of the cutter with big deadrise, deep hull and convex entrance lines. James M. Hilhouse built numerous fast-sailing schooners and small square riggers at Bristol in the years 1790–1822 giving them steep deadrise and fine lines. The type of mail packet and fruit schooner he produced was probably typical of the early clippers built in Great Britain in the first quarter of the nineteenth century.

In the years 1825–40, it is more difficult to establish the trend of design for fast-sailing ships as the carriage of cargo was all-important and ships required for speed were largely confined to the fruit and opium trades, to a few mail packets which also carried passengers, and to yachts.

After 1823, the British Post Office packet service was controlled by the Admiralty who tended to replace the privately-built craft with naval vessels. The brig *Neilson* which was built at Buckler's Hard in 1824 of 232 tons is a typical example of a vessel built in these years for trade to South America and the West Indies. She has some deadrise with a convex entrance to the hull but a finer hollow run, and is a moderately deep vessel. She did not set skysails. In 1827 she took 44 days from Deal to Trinidad.

Some large yachts were built at this date to try and encourage the Admiralty to improve the sailing performance of warships. The members of the Royal Yacht Squadron had definite ideas of speed at sea. Lord Yarborough's ship-rigged yacht *Falcon* was built in 1824, and lines taken off a model in the Science Museum show that she had very steep deadrise with fine convex waterlines in the hull. She had a tonnage of 351. Later, under the ownership of Baring Brothers, the *Falcon* carried tea back from China to the London market in 1837–8, because Baring's considered her a 'fast' ship. Subsequently she was in the opium trade.

---

* Lubbock, *Last of the Windjammers*, Vol I, pp. 187–8.

[**Above**] *This model is entitled* Emma *of Sidmouth but no actual schooner has so far been identified with it. It represents a typical Baltimore clipper schooner that was being built prior to 1815, and the absence of a windlass suggests a warship rather than a merchant vessel.* (Science Museum).

[**Below**] *Lines plan of the three-masted French privateer* L'Intrepide *designed for Citizen Elizé Nairac and drawn by Guibert snr, probably in about 1790–1810. The very steep deadrise is clearly shown in the body plan on the left; the pumps are drawn just abaft the mainmast; there is a plain gammon knee.* (Mariner's Museum, Newport News).

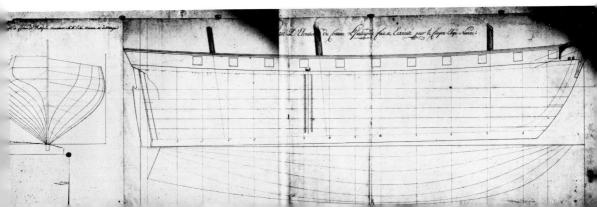

[**Above**] *A model of the Post Office packet* Duke of Marlborough *as made by her carpenter in 1814 and presented to her commander, Captain John Bull. This packet brig was built at Falmouth in 1806 and was of 180 tons. Still afloat in 1821, she sailed from Lisbon to Falmouth in 5 days in the Spring of that year, making a round trip every month.* (Parker Gallery).

[**Opposite top**] *The* Falcon *when under Jardine Matheson's colours, seen in the China Sea. She was built in 1824 as Lord Yarborough's yacht. With the sails on the foremast aback and shaking, she has presumably just gone about, and the fore yard is about to be hauled round.* (Author).

[**Opposite bottom**] *A sail plan of the American schooner* Fly *which was captured by the Royal Navy in 1811 and renamed H M S* Sea Lark. *Place and date of build unknown, but she is a typical Baltimore clipper. Plan drawn by David R. MacGregor.* (Author).

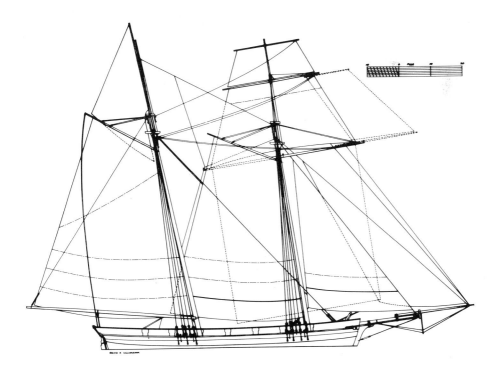

CHAPTER THREE

Early Clipper Ships 1830-1850

In the two decades leading up to 1850, the development of the China trade and the carriage of opium called for fast ships of clipper build. Although trade to Chinese ports was still restricted to Canton until after the Anglo-Chinese War of 1839–42, a need was growing for ships to replace the lordly East Indiamen, whose monopoly of trade to China was terminated in 1834. The Indiamen often made passages home in less than 120 days with the monsoon behind them, and it was in an endeavour to maintain these passages that ships were built for the trade or brought into it. The added spur of competition also required faster ships.

It was related in the last chapter how the *Falcon* was possibly one of the earliest clippers to have loaded tea for the London markets. Other British ships engaged in the trade in the 1830s included the *Alexander Baring, John o'Gaunt, Euphrates, James Matheson, Mangles* and *Bonanza*. The first four were all built between 1834 and 1836 as a result of the opening of trade to all comers, but no plans are known by which their claim as clippers can be verified. The *Alexander Baring* was called a 'fast sailer' by her owners, Baring Brothers, who had her built at the Blackwall Yard in London, in 1834, of 612 tons n.m. The *John o'Gaunt* was built at Liverpool in 1835 by John Wilson of 449 tons and enjoyed a great reputation for speed under the command of Captain John Robertson who later commanded the tea clippers *Stornoway* and *Cairngorm*. She is reputed to have sailed out to Anjer in less than 66 days on one occasion; in 1838 she took 88 days to get there from Liverpool.

The last two ships of the six named above, the *Mangles* and *Bonanza*, were built prior to 1834; the former was constructed at Calcutta in 1802 and claimed a run of 94 days between London and Macao in 1829; the latter was built at Whitehaven by Thomas Brocklebank in 1830 and took 91 days between Shanghai and Liverpool in 1844. This sort of passage was real clipper ship stuff. The *Bonanza* was a brig of 176 tons and was a longer and finer-lined version of the Brocklebank brigantine *Dash* (1828). (Plans of the *Dash* formed figures 70 and 71 of my book, *Fast Sailing Ships*.) Brocklebank ships were painted black outside the hull with a broad white band just below the sheer strake; inboard, the bulwarks and deck fittings were coloured green, and so was the base of each mast to a height equivalent to the height of the bulwarks.

Another Brocklebank ship built for the China trade in 1833 was the *Jumna* of 364 tons which in 1834–35 made a passage of 102 days between Canton and Liverpool. This ship had an unusual life, being bought by Dundee owners in 1856 when she was converted into a whaler; in 1863 she was fitted with engines but was crushed in the ice the same year in Arctic waters.

[**Above**] *With a light breeze, the brig* Governor Maclean *stands off the Fort of Annamboe on the Gold Coast, North Africa, where she went for palm oil and ivory. Built in 1833 at Millwall on the Thames, she registered 252 tons. She had to be armed to defend herself and heavily rigged because of adverse weather and to escape pursuit. Excessive rake to the masts was then considered advantageous for a fast ship. Here she has some stunsails set, but the large fore trysail is brailed into the mast.* (Parker Gallery).

[**Below**] *The opium clipper* Omega *was built at Cowes in 1837 of 178 tons. Here she is hove-to, her crew standing by her 'long tom' in the bows as the Chinese junks approach. Although a schooner, she could set square topsails, topgallants and royals on each mast, and her topgallant mast on the fore is fidded. With such long lower masts, she cannot be a brig. Chalk drawing by J. G. Hely dated 29 September 1845.* (National Maritime Museum).

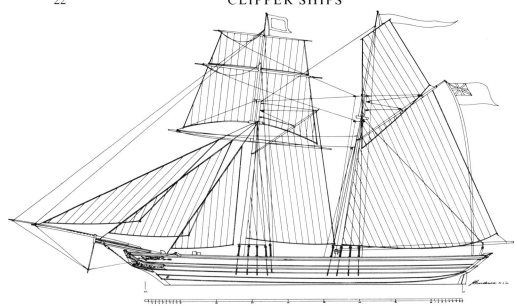

[**Above**] *Sail plan of the Aberdeen clipper schooner* Matchless, *built in 1846 of 107 tons for trade between Leith and Lerwick. She cost £2000. The sails and rigging are reconstructed, but the spar dimensions are listed. Drawn by James Henderson.* (Author).

[**Below**] *Lines plan of the schooner* Matchless *built at Aberdeen in 1846 by Alexander Hall & Sons of 107 tons, with dimensions of 89.0 ft × 18.0 ft × 11.4 ft. Drawn by James Henderson.* (Author).

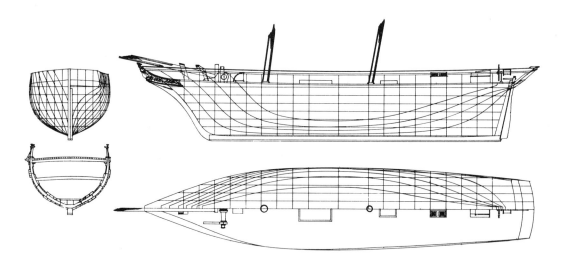

In *Greyhounds of the Sea*, Carl C. Cutler has referred to the fast passages of less than 100 days being made with a fair degree of regularity between Canton and Boston or New York in the 1830s, one of the fastest being made in 1834 by the *Sabina* which reached Sandy Hook 90 days from Canton.

In 1833 the full-rigged ship *Ann McKim* was built at Baltimore on extremely sharp lines to a design that was really an enlarged Baltimore clipper schooner with dimensions of 143 ft (between perpendiculars) × 31 ft (moulded) × 15 ft 10 ins (moulded), and she had a drag aft of about 5 ft. She was a fast ship and entered the China trade in 1839. But due to all the other fast ships that had preceded her, it can now be shown, once and for all, that she has no right to be called the first clipper ship. Some of her passages were quite lengthy, as was occasionally the case with ships of extreme clipper build, although in 1843 she came home from Canton in 96 days.

Ann McKim's design is more of the style to be expected in an opium clipper, as this trade attracted some interesting craft, including those which formerly were warships, slavers, fruiters and yachts. The carrying of opium from India to the China coast was dramatically altered in 1830 when the American barque *Red Rover*, whose design was said to have been based on the privateer *Prince de Neuchâtel*, beat up the China Sea against the monsoon to complete a passage of only 22 days from Singapore to Macao. A boom followed in the building of clippers to carry this cargo, which had to be smuggled ashore into China. Many fine clippers were built in Bombay or Calcutta, including the *Sylph*, *Waterwitch*, *Cowasjee Family*, *Rob Roy*, *Ariel*, *Lady Grant* and others. *Lady Grant* was described as 'the very extreme of sharpness'.* The *Waterwitch* was designed by Captain Andrew Henderson and built at Calcutta in 1831, having a very broad hull with dimensions of 104 ft 11 in × 27 ft 10 in × 17 ft 6 in and 363 tons. One wonders if Henderson was influenced by the cutter hull-form? Sir Robert Seppings designed *Sylph* and *Cowasjee Family* for a Calcutta merchant, but unfortunately none of these plans have survived. From contemporary pictures, it appears that all these clippers had very lofty masts on which was set a cloud of canvas. A picture in *Fast Sailing Ships* (figure 89), thought to be of *Waterwitch*, shows the barque actually setting a big crossjack from a yard on her mizen.

Some big yachts became opium clippers, such as the brig *Anonyma* which was built in 1839 at Gosport by William Camper of 459 tons. She was still influenced by the cutter hull as her great beam of 29 ft 10 ins gave her less than four beams to length. But the hull was much shallower than the usual cutter-build, in spite of steep deadrise and fine lines. She had a lofty rig, setting skysails on each of her heavily raked masts, and she was a large vessel to be rigged as a brig. At this date, vessels built for speed usually had a big rise of floor but without the extremely long, sharp entrance and run found in the clippers after 1850.

For clippers sailing up the China Sea against the north-east monsoon, a total length of passage from the Sand Heads off Calcutta to Lintin at the mouth of the Canton River was considered fast if it approached 40 days. With the south-west monsoon behind them, clippers could take 20 days less. For instance, in 1832 the *Waterwitch* took 21 days from the Sand Heads to Lintin and the *Sylph* took only 18 days in the same year, 14 August to 1 September.

The first full-rigged ship built in Great Britain for the opium trade, according to Basil Lubbock's list in *The Opium Clippers*, was the *Mor* of 280 tons built in London in 1840 to the order of Jardine Matheson. On her maiden passage she took only 81 days to

* Basil Lubbock, *The Opium Clippers*, p. 118.

Anjer from London and was always spoken of as a very fast ship.

Without the backing of plans or builders' models, it becomes a matter of speculation as to the relative merits of various so-called clippers, but a line of more sound development can be found in tracing the progress of the clippers built at Aberdeen by Alexander Hall & Sons, where the builder's account book has survived as well as spar dimensions and half-models. Hall's shipyard received an order from a group of Aberdonians to build a schooner that would compete with the ships of the Aberdeen & London Steam Navigation Co on the Aberdeen to London route, and in 1839 they launched the *Scottish Maid* with an experimental form of bow—experimental, that is to say, to Aberdonians. This schooner was liked immediately, especially as she occasionally made the trip between the two ports in forty-nine hours. She cost £1700 and her measurements were 92.4 ft × 19.4 ft × 11.4 ft, 142 tons n.m. and 195 ton o.m. It will be recalled in Chapter One how a vessel could be deemed to be fine-lined if the new measurement (n.m.) tonnage figure was significantly less than the old measurement (o.m.) figure.

The *Scottish Maid* was a sharp model schooner with considerable deadrise, slack bilges, a long convex entrance and a fairly long concave run. The masts were raked well aft and placed close together, and the foremast was a good distance from the bows. One result of raking the stem forward to form the cutwater was that the effective length on deck was increased, which in turn brought the positions where two of the three sets of tonnage measurements were taken, closer to bow and stern where the cross-sectional areas were naturally smaller. This had the anomaly of reducing the tonnage by increasing the length! The matter is discussed in great detail in Chapter Four of *Fast Sailing Ships*. Thus a loophole was found in the 1836 Tonnage Law which simultaneously aided the design of fine-lined vessels. In fairness to the new rule, it should be added that a ship's depth was now actually measured for tonnage, it having previously been assumed to be half the depth! Indeed, this wild assumption had done much to produce the deep-hulled ships built in British yards; although conversely, in America, the same assumption applied, yet it did not prevent the building of extreme clippers, especially as the American rules remained unchanged until 1864.

Commencing with the *Scottish Maid*, thirty-six vessels were built in Hall's yard with his 'Aberdeen bow' up to and including the ship *Bonita* of 1848 out of a total number of sixty-five craft. It was quite an achievement that so many were built in this new fashion because not every owner wanted this sort of bow nor even a clipper hull.

The first opium clipper built by Hall was the *Torrington* of 1845, and plans of the schooner *Matchless* which he built the following year are reproduced here. She was a natural development from the *Scottish Maid* in which the basic essentials of the original design were but little changed. The first three-masted square rigger with the raking stem was the *Colloony* of 1844, measuring 287 tons n.m. and 335 tons o.m.; her stem raked forward 21 ft from the fore end of the keel. The first full-rigged ship to this design was undoubtedly the *Bon Accord*, built in 1846 for trade to the East.

It was not long before other builders both in Aberdeen and other parts of the country began giving their latest creations their own version of the 'Aberdeen bow'. Laird Brothers at Birkenhead built the iron schooner *Proto* as early as 1841 with this form of bow, giving her rounded floors and slack bilges, with a very hollow entrance and run,

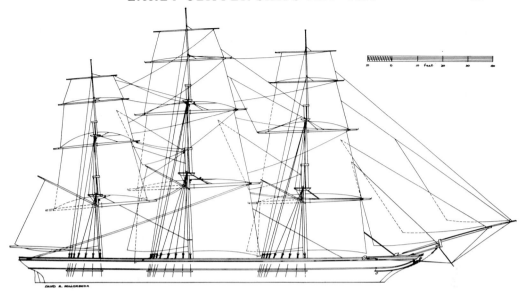

[**Above**] *This sail plan of the Aberdeen clipper* Reindeer *is reconstructed from the listed spar dimensions. Standing trysail gaffs on the fore and main masts were common before 1850. One feature is the great length of the poles above the royal yards, but no skysail yards are listed by the builder.* (Author).

[**Below**] *Lines plan of the* Reindeer *built at Aberdeen in 1848 by Alexander Hall & Sons of 328 tons, with dimensions of 141.5 ft × 22.7 ft × 15.5 ft. The lines were taken off the builders' half-model in the Glasgow Museum. Plan drawn by David R. MacGregor.* (Author).

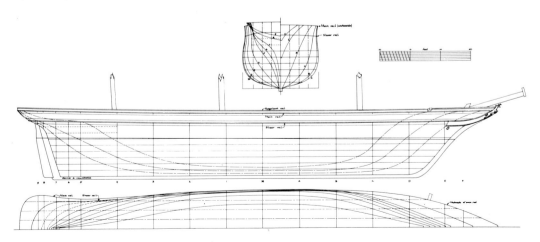

as a surviving lines plan proves. Walter Hood's yard at Aberdeen produced about a dozen such clippers in the 1840s and Alexander Duthie's yard came second with eight. The Lloyd's Register surveyor at Aberdeen often described the bow in such terms as: 'flared out bow termed clipper carried to an extreme'. This was in the case of Hall's barque *Emperor* of 1849. At Dumbarton, William Denny built four iron clipper schooners between 1846–51 of which the first, the *Annsbro'*, was fitted with a centreboard working on a pivot.

Towards the end of the forties, some remarkable ships were built in Aberdeen on clipper lines, and surviving half-models show that Hall's clippers *Reindeer* (1848 of 328 tons n.m. and 427 tons o.m.), and *Benjamin Elkin* (1849 of 367 tons n.m. and 425 tons o.m.) were both of extreme clipper form and of broadly similar hull-form, although the former was some 7 ft longer. Above a good deadrise, Hall favoured flaring topsides at this date, which was an unusual feature; the entrance was straight at the load line but hollow below, and there was a long run. But there is a curious feature in the shape of *Reindeer*'s stern which suddenly swells out on the quarter before curving round. *Benjamin Elkin* and an unnamed model in Hall's offices also have this queer stern, which modern naval architects find unaccountable. *Reindeer*'s dimensions are 141.5 ft × 22.7 ft × 15.5 ft. Her sail plan was not particularly large; trysail gaffs are specified for each mast, and although the royal poles extend a fair height above the yards, no skysails are listed. *Reindeer* was probably one of the finest-lined clippers that had been built in Great Britain up to this time. On her first passage home, she took 106 days with the fair monsoon between Whampoa and Liverpool in 1849–50; later in 1850 she sailed home against the monsoon in 107 days between Hong Kong and Liverpool, 20 August to 5 December.

Benjamin Elkin was an expensively built ship costing £15 per ton; her deck fittings were of polished mahogany and many of her timbers were of the same material. Hulls of Aberdeen ships were often painted a darkish greeny-blue.

At Walter Hood's yard, the barque *Phoenician* (1847) and the full-rigged ships *Oliver Cromwell* and *John Bunyan* (both 1848) were all probably built to the same hull-form as their dimensions were so similar. *Oliver Cromwell* forms an average: 148.5 ft × 27.3 ft × 18.7 ft; 478 tons n.m. and 527 tons o.m. *Phoenician* was 1.5 ft shorter and *John Bunyan* 1.8 ft longer. On her second China passage, *John Bunyan* left Shanghai on 28th January 1850 and passed Deal 101 days later, bound for London. It was later declared that she was only 98 or 99 days from land to land or between her pilots; but these claims only came out towards the end of that year when the American clipper *Oriental* of over twice her tonnage had docked in London 97 days out from Hong Kong, having passed the Lizard when only 91 days out. British patriots were encouraged by the passage of the Scots clipper at a time when they thought the Yankee clippers were about to sweep the board after the repeal of the Navigation Laws in 1849. But the differences in size, season of sailing and port of departure really make any rational comparison an impossibility. The *Oriental* is discussed later in this chapter.

Other British clippers built at the end of the forties included *Sea Witch* built 1848 in London for the China trade; *Watkins* built in 1848 at Newhaven; and *Ocean Queen* (1846), *Countess of Seafield* (1848) and *Shepherdess* (1850), all three of which were built at Aberdeen by John Duthie.

After the Anglo-Chinese War in 1842, Hong Kong was ceded to Great Britain and a number of ports were opened to foreign trade, but the Navigation Laws prevented tea being brought to British ports in anything except British ships.

[**Above**] *The* Ocean Queen *forms a good example of an Aberdeen clipper barque, with a large forward rake to her stem. She was built in 1846 by John Duthie, and was of 349 tons. This painting is by J. Heard.* (Parker Gallery).

[**Below**] *The artist E. J. Gregory has portrayed the clipper brig* Granite *under close-reefed topsails and reefed courses. She was built at Aberdeen by Walter Hood in 1846 with a tonnage of 186 and was owned in the port.* (Author).

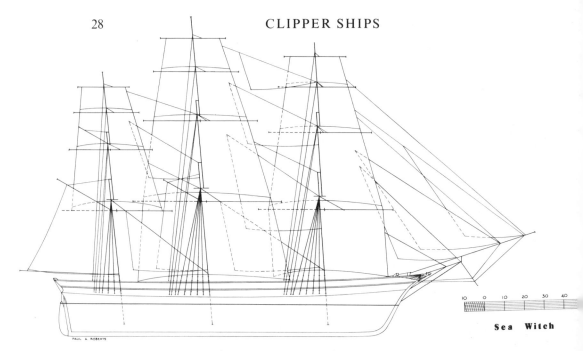

Sea   Witch

[**Above**] *The American clipper* Sea Witch, *built in 1846, was much larger than the Aberdeen clippers, being almost three times the tonnage of* Reindeer. *This plan was drawn by Paul Roberts from one in the Smithsonian Institution; the staysails, main trysail and jibs have been reconstructed.* (Author).

[**Below**] *The lines plan of the* Sea Witch. *She was designed by J. W. Griffiths and built at New York in 1846 by Smith & Dimon, and measured 178 ft 2 in × 33 ft 0 in × 21 ft 6 in and 907 tons. Plan reconstructed by Paul Roberts from drawing in Smithsonian Institution.* (Author).

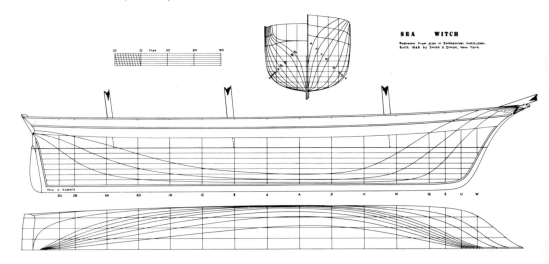

SEA   WITCH

Redrawn from plan in Smithsonian Institution.
Built 1846 by Smith & Dimon, New York.

The trans-Atlantic passenger trade also demanded fast ships but as the packets had to sail on schedule in winter as well as summer, they were obliged to be very seaworthy and strongly built, and for this reason their hull-form tended to be of the flat-bottomed deep-sided type, but with moderately fine ends. They possessed great power to carry sail in strong winds and their determined masters ensured that they did so. Plans of packet ships built at New York by Isaac Webb and his son, William, have survived. From such models, William Webb developed the ships sent out to China via the Cape of Good Hope; they had greater deadrise than the Atlantic packet ships, as well as finer waterlines, particularly in the run. The *Helena* of 1841 was the first of these 'China packets', and in 1844 she took 90 days between Canton and New York. He followed her with such ships as *Panama* and *Montauk* which made some good passages, but they remained deep ships in relation to their length, *Montauk*'s dimensions being 128 ft 9 in length on deck, 29 ft 0½ in breadth moulded and 19 ft 0 in depth of hold.

A word should be said here about Isaac Webb and his influence on the clipper ship. He had been apprentice, foreman and finally successor to Henry Eckford at his New York yard. He had the ability to impart his knowledge and three of his apprentices became leading ship designers: his eldest son, William; John W. Griffiths; and Donald McKay. Each of these three left their mark on the clipper ship era.

From 1843, Griffiths lectured on his theories of improved naval architecture for fast-sailing ships, of which the principal points were to rake the stem forward above the load line—the success of the Aberdeen bow in this respect was not mentioned; to introduce hollows in the waterlines at the ends; and to raise the level of the quarters by reducing the overhang of the stern. He designed the clipper ship *Rainbow* which Smith & Dimon built in New York in 1845 for Howland & Aspinall. She was really an elongated version of a China packet with more hollows in the ends and a much longer run. On her sail plan, moonsails are drawn on each mast. Her measurements were 159 ft 0 in × 31 ft 10 in × 18 ft 4 in and 752 tons. *Rainbow* was hardly afloat before one of the firm's other ships, the *Natchez*, under Captain Robert Waterman, reached New York only 78 days out from Macao, a remarkable performance for a fourteen-year-old trans-Atlantic packet. Howland & Aspinall determined to build for Waterman the fastest clipper they could and commissioned Griffiths accordingly.

John Griffiiths was apparently given *carte blanche* to design the fastest ship he could, and Smith & Dimon built her. The result was the *Sea Witch* built in 1846 with dimensions of 178 ft 2 in (on deck) × 33 ft 0 in (moulded) × 21 ft 6 in (moulded), and 907 tons. In design she had departed from many of the packet ship features and now exhibited more of the clipper ship hull-form to be seen from 1850 onwards. Her raking stem rabbet was akin to the clippers being built in Aberdeen, although her bowsprit did not spring from the hull in the same manner. She had a very hollow entrance and as the midship section was kept well forward of the centre of her hull, there was a long convex run. There was good deadrise with very slack bilges and hardly any tumblehome. In her sail plan, skysails are not drawn above the royals.

She proved to be a very fast ship under Captain Waterman and her fastest passages are listed here:

1846	New York to Java Head	23 Dec to 4 Mar 1847	71 days
	(passage continued to Canton)		
1847	Canton to New York	3 May to 25 July	83 days
	was only 62 days from Anjer		

The American clipper Oriental *as pictured in the* Illustrated London News *in December 1850 after her arrival from China. She was probably the largest clipper that had ever visited the River Thames. She was built at New York in 1849 of 1003 tons.* (Author).

THE SHIP "ORIENTAL," OF NEW YORK.

1847	Canton to New York	29 Dec to 15 Mar 1848	77 days
1849	Hong Kong to New York	9 Jan to 25 Mar	75 days
	was only 7 days to Anjer		
1850	New York to Valparaiso	13 April to 11 June	59 days

passage continued to San Francisco, arrived 24 July being 97 days under sail. This last passage was under Captain G. W. Fraser.

Her two passages from China of 75 and 77 days—calculated to the nearest day—have never been beaten, but it is important to note that they were both made with the favourable north-east monsoon. On the other hand, her run of 83 days on her maiden voyage was made against the monsoon, which made this passage exceptionally fast. Ships bound to England were estimated by Matthew F. Maury to take an extra 12 days on the passage after crossing the Line in the North Atlantic, so fans of British clipper records can take comfort in this. The clippers being currently produced in Aberdeen were less than half the size of ships like *Sea Witch* so that their speed potential was that much less.

In 1847, Brown & Bell of New York built the *Samuel Russell* of 957 tons for the China trade, with big deadrise and sharp lines; her fastest passage was one of 81 days from Canton to New York in 1848. A year later, Jacob Bell, who had succeeded Brown & Bell, built the *Oriental* on fairly similar lines but with less deadrise. She ran in the tea trade to London for several years and was reported to have sailed at 16 knots. After her arrival in London in December 1850, her lines were taken off in Green's Blackwall Yard in the following January.

The only plans so far found of a British ship with equivalent hull-form to these China packets are of the *Camertonian* which was built at Workington in 1848 of 485 tons o.m. Her lines, taken from a contemporary model, were published in *Fast Sailing Ships*. She was somewhat similar to Webb's *Helena*.

From hulls developed from the trans-Atlantic packets came these 'China packets' and indeed the term 'packet model' was applied in America to describe a clipper with flat floors and high vertical sides. Such a form was in direct contrast to the 'Baltimore' or 'pilot boat' model.

For Sale,

THE BEAUTIFUL NEW BARQUE

ECHO,

$422\frac{7}{10}$ Tons new measurement, and $376\frac{72}{94}$ Tons old measurement;

Length 114 feet; Breadth 26 feet 9 inches; Depth 18 feet 6 inches.

She was built by Messrs. JOSEPH CUNARD & Co. at Miramichi, (New Brunswick), under the superintendence of Mr. WILLIAM RENNIE, whose Ships are well known. She is composed entirely of hackmatack or larch, with the exception of the flooring, and is copper-fastened; has a raised quarter-deck and figure-head, is abundantly fastened, and finished off in the very best manner. No expense or labour having been spared to make her a very superior Ship.

LYING IN THE WEST INDIA SOUTH DOCK.

Hull, Masts, Yards, Standing and Running Rigging, with all faults, as they now lie.

INVENTORY.

ANCHORS.

1 best bower
1 small do.
1 stream
1 kedge

CABLES.

2 chain cables
2 bending shackles
3 warps

SAILS.

1 standing jib
1 fore-top-mast staysail
1 fore sail
1 fore-top sail
1 fore-top gallant sail
1 square main sail
1 main-topsail
1 main-top-gallant sail
1 mizen

CARPENTER'S & BOATSWAIN'S STORES.

4 pump spears
2 do. brakes
1 do. hook
4 do. bolts
4 lower pump boxes
1 lb. spare pump leather
1 spare top-gallant mast
1 do. topsail yard

4 top-mast studding-sail booms
2 top-gallant do. do.
2 lower do. do.
1 spare top-mast
1 do. lower yard
6 steering-sail yards
2 tarpaulins
12 capstan bars
10 handspikes
1 long boat
1 skiff, rudder, and tiller
1 do. davit
12 oars
1 spun yarn
1 top block
1 cat block
1 anchor fish hook
4 double luff tackle blocks
4 single do. do.
1 bit stopper
2 marline spikes
2 serving mallets
1 watch tackle
2 boats' chocks
3 fenders
$\frac{1}{2}$ cask of stockholm tar

COOPER'S STORES.

13 water casks
1 harness cask
6 flour barrels
2 kegs

3 buckets
6 mess kits

SHIP'S CHANDLER STORES.

1 brass compass
1 wood do.
4 log glasses
1 log-reel line
1 deep sea lead line
1 deep sea lead
1 hand lead
1 hand lead line
1 signal lantern
1 ensign, jack
2 deck and paint scrubbing brushes
1 scraper
1 keg of whitelead

CABIN STORES.

1 tea kettle
2 dishes
6 plates
2 saucepans
1 candlestick
2 tin steamers
1 brass cabin stove and funnel
1 cask of bread
$\frac{1}{2}$ do. of beef

COOK'S STORES.

1 cabouse
1 frying pan
1 cook's ladle
1 pair tormentors
1 cook's lantern

The Vessel and her Stores to be taken with all faults as they now lie, without any allowance for weight, length quality, or any deficiency whatever, or any error in description.

Inventories and further particulars known by applying to

THOMAS CARTER,

Mill Wall Dock, Mill Wall.

This is a typical ship's inventory. The Echo *was built in 1842 and the following year was owned in Jersey by Quetville. Her builder, Rennie, later designed many fine tea clippers such as* Fiery Cross *and* Norman Court. *(I. Barling).*

CHAPTER FOUR

British Clippers of the 1850's

Although the peak of tea clipper production was achieved during the sixties, the greatest boom for the design and building of all classes of clippers occurred during the previous decade, and of this period it was during the years 1853–1855 that the greatest number of clippers were launched. The two principal causes which stimulated the demand for clippers in Great Britain were the competition with American ships, following the repeal of the Navigation Acts in 1849, and the discovery of gold in Australia two years later.

One of the principal differences between British and American clippers was one of size; American ships were usually larger and also were built exclusively of wood. Whereas in the 1850s there were only three British clippers larger than 1,500 tons—the *Schomberg*, *Tayleur* and *Eastern Monarch*—there were over 70 in America and twelve of these exceeded 2,000 tons each. But although the giant *Sovereign of the Seas* of 2,420 tons was an ideal ship for rounding Cape Horn with passengers and selected cargo for the Californian goldfields, she was not suited to the China tea trade where the ports were unaccustomed to filling the immense holds of large ships. Here the smaller British ships of 400 to 800 tons were ideally suited, besides which they were easier to navigate in poorly charted rivers and harbours along the China coast. Careful examination of many plans and models of such clippers prove that British ships were not mere copies of their American rivals but were designed independently as the result of specific trade requirements which differed in each country. In addition, the use of iron for the fabric of the hull produced an altogether different type of design to the American model, and some of the most extreme versions of the clipper were indeed built of iron.

The largest clipper ever built in Great Britain was the *Schomberg* which was launched in 1855 from Alexander Hall's yard in Aberdeen. She registered 2,284 tons and had dimensions of 247.7 ft × 45.5 ft × 28.9 ft. She was diagonally planked with four layers which resulted in a minimum thickness of $13\frac{1}{2}$ in, and this permitted a wider spacing of the frames. There were four decks with 60 staterooms and she was said to be capable of carrying a thousand passengers. She was a very fine-lined ship though with average deadrise, but she had an immense sail plan with five square sails on each mast. The main lower yard was no less than 111 ft 6 in long, being the longest yard ever fitted to a British merchant sailing ship. She was ordered by James Baines of Liverpool as the British counterpart to the big clippers he had bought from Donald McKay of Boston, but unfortunately she was wrecked on the Australian coast at the end of her maiden passage. Her longest run in 24 hours was 368 miles.

The development of the raking Aberdeen stem in the 1840s gave additional stimulus

A spirited lithograph by T. G. Dutton of the Aberdeen clipper Schomberg *outward bound on her maiden passage to Australia in 1855. She was by far the largest clipper ever built in Great Britain but was wrecked at the end of her maiden passage. Her lower and topsail yards were especially long.* (Parker Gallery).

to clipper ship building and many of Hall's ships were built on this model, of which *Reindeer*, *Cairngorm* and *Vision* were all extreme versions but all different in hull-form; *Stornoway*, *Chrysolite* and *Robin Hood* were some of Hall's less extreme clippers. All these six vessels were built for the tea trade, and all were full-rigged ships. *Stornoway*, built in 1850, for Jardine, Matheson & Co, is often looked on as the first real British tea clipper, partly because ships such as *Reindeer* and *John Bunyan* were on the small side. *Stornoway* was of 527 tons n.m. and her fastest homeward passage was probably 104 days between Whampoa and London in 1851, made against the monsoon. An indication of how important the master was, can be seen in the passages of the *Chrysolite*: under Anthony Enright, who had come from the *Reindeer* and was soon to be master of the *Lightning*, her first four homeward passages averaged $105\frac{1}{4}$ days from China; her second four passages under Alexander McLelland averaged 135 days. What a difference! As a result of the slower passages, the ship was probably loaded at £1 per ton less in freight than under Enright.

The *Robin Hood*, built by Hall in 1856 of 852 tons, was a fast ship and claimed to have sailed 364 miles in 24 hours on her first voyage, which is 34 miles faster than *Thermopylae*'s best. Homeward-bound from Foochow in 1862, she damaged her rudder, but Captain John Mann brought her safely home and received a bonus of £100 from the owner, James Beazley, paid in gold sovereigns. The money was left in a bag on a table in the hotel. When Captain Mann returned, he found that his children had pushed most of the sovereigns down the cracks between the floor boards, which had to be taken up to recover the money.

An interesting point about the *Cairngorm*'s design is that it was not dictated by an owner's requirements but embodied the builder's convictions of the ideal tea clipper that could compete on equal terms with the Americans. It was a bold decision to construct such a specialized ship on speculation without first obtaining a firm order, but Alexander Hall & Sons were proved right because, after the *Cairngorm* was bought by Jardine, Matheson & Co, she turned out to be one of the fastest clippers in the tea trade during the fifties. She had very fine lines and extremely steep rise of floor above hollow garboards. Compared with the American clipper ship plans reproduced by Howard I. Chapelle in *Search for Speed under Sail* only *Samuel Russell* (1847) has so much deadrise, but without the hollow garboards and with fuller ends. *Cairngorm*'s measurements were: 939 tons n.m. and 1246 o.m.; 193.3 ft × 36.6 ft × 20.2 ft. With such a fine hull, an extra tall sail plan was not necessary; instead it was very 'square'. She cost £15,434 to build which is about £700 less than the *Cutty Sark*'s original cost; on 939 tons, every ton cost £16.43 which is incredibly cheap by today's standards.

Described as the 'Cock of the Walk', *Cairngorm* made some fast passages such as her maiden trip of 72 days in 1853 from Lisbon to Hong Kong under Captain Robertson. She had put into Lisbon partially dismasted. Her fastest homeward passage from China

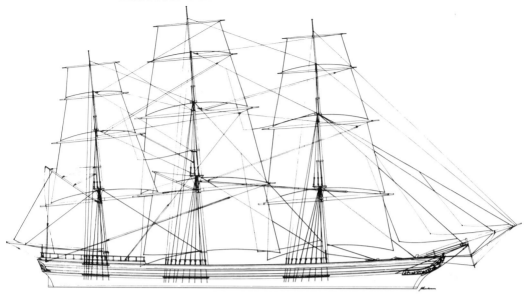

[**Above**] *Sail plan of the clipper* Cairngorm, *built in 1853 by A. Hall & Sons at Aberdeen. With extremely sharp lines, the sail area is not excessive, but stunsails would have been set in fair winds, as well as a flying jib and royal staysails. This plan is reconstructed by James Henderson from the builder's spar dimensions.* (Author).

[**Opposite**] *A model of the Aberdeen clipper* Stornoway *which was built in 1850 by Alexander Hall & Sons of 527 tons and a length of 157.8 ft. This model, made by James Henderson, is based on the builder's half-model and spar dimensions, but the deck fittings and rigging are reconstructed. Curiously, no mizen skysail mast is listed.* (James Henderson).

[**Below**] *Lines plan of the extreme clipper* Cairngorm, *built at Aberdeen in 1853 by A. Hall & Sons, with measurements of 193.3 ft × 33.6 ft × 20.2 ft and 939 tons n.m. Lines taken off builder's half-model in Glasgow Museum and drawn out by David R MacGregor.* (Author).

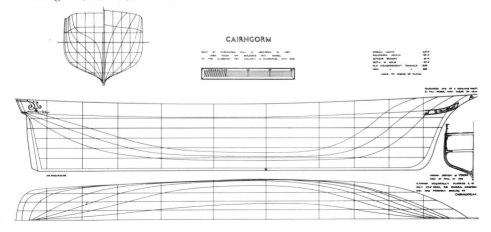

CAIRNGORM

lasted 91 days when she raced back to Deal from Macao in 1858–59, beating William
Pile's clipper *Lammermuir* by one day.

Two other builders risked their reputation by designing and constructing their
concept of an ideal clipper. These were Alexander Stephen & Sons, builders of *Storm
Cloud* and *White Eagle*, and Benjamin Nicholson who built *Annandale*. These four
ships were probably amongst the finest-lined clippers ever built in Great Britain.

Benjamin Nicholson's shipyard was at Annan on the north side of the Solway Firth,
and here he built the clippers *Annandale*, *Queensberry*, *Shakspere* and *Mansfield*
between 1854 and 1861; his other ships were carriers or medium clippers. *Annandale*
was also notable for her great length in proportion to breadth, her measurements being
226.9 ft × 31.8 ft × 18.5 ft, 759 tons n.m. and 1,131 tons o.m. This makes her ratio 7.1
beams to length. *Queensberry*'s ratio was 7.2 to 1. The greatest ratio was probably in
the iron clipper *Tempest* (1855) with 7.5 to 1. All the ships built by Benjamin Nicholson
were owned by a family firm and managed in Liverpool by Nicholson & McGill.

Under Captain Crockett, *Annandale* did not make any exceptionally fast passages
apart from taking only 7 days to sail from Singapore to Hong Kong in 1856. The
captain claimed that in the previous year she sailed a noon-to-noon distance of 381
miles during which she made 18 knots. This speed, on a load line length of 220 ft 4 in,

The extreme iron clipper Pareora ex White Eagle *photographed in New Zealand. She was
built in 1855 by A. Stephen & Sons at Glasgow and measured 879 tons net. The angle of
the painted ports in the bows gives some idea of the long sharp entrance.* (Alexander
Turnbull Library).

gives a speed–length ratio of 1.22, indicating a fast ship. Nicholson's sold her in 1860 and five years later she went ashore at Key West, America.

The other builders to produce an ideal clipper were Alexander Stephen & Sons who built the *Storm Cloud* in 1854 and the *White Eagle* a year later. Both these ships were designed on John Scott Russell's 'Wave Line Theory', which was first propounded by this naval architect in 1842–43. He was interested in wave-making resistance which hindered a ship's passage through the water above a certain speed. His theories resulted in a long concave entrance and a shorter but concave run; the latter was to be only two-third's the length of the entrance. In *Storm Cloud*, the fullest part of the hull is abreast of the mainmast, and her long hollow entrance is surely unique. The half-model which used to hang on the stairs of Stephen's office resembled a very fine-lined yacht, not a ship to carry cargo. Her dimensions were 201.6 ft × 33.0 ft × 20.3 ft and 798 tons net; her coefficient of under-deck tonnage is .51, which is the lowest yet found for a clipper. *White Eagle* was 90 tons larger.

A book by the American naval architect, John W. Griffiths, entitled *Treatise on Marine and Naval Architecture*, was listed by Alexander Stephen Jnr in his notebook; Griffiths approved of the design of the yacht *America* with her long, sharp concave entrance, but he denied that Scott Russell's theories had had any influence on the

Many of the iron clippers, such as the Lord of the Isles, *pictured here in Chinese waters, had practically no sheer, and possessed the sharp lines of a steamer. She was built on the Clyde in 1853 of 691 tons. As she is close-hauled on the starboard tack, the stunsails are not set and the booms are hauled in below the yards, but her jibs and staysails are particularly large. Her topsails are fitted with Cunningham's roller-reefing gear.* (Alexander Turnbull Library).

Seen here in the River Thames, the Wynaud *was originally built as a full-rigged ship for the opium trade but instead became a tea clipper. She was built at Rotherhithe in 1854 and was of 546 tons. Beginning at the mainmast and stretching forward of the foremast are two spare masts lashed down on top of the deckhouse. There is another deckhouse between the main and mizen masts.* (National Maritime Museum).

concave lines in American clippers. Not only were British ship designers undeniably initiating original clippers but the possibility of their influence spreading across the Atlantic was being hotly denied.

A factor that should not be overlooked is that all Stephen's clippers were built of iron which was a material not employed in American clippers. This material required a far thinner shell or sides and removed the forest-like structure needed to stiffen and maintain the shape inside a large wooden ship. The cargo capacity of an iron ship of 500 tons increased by 16% over one built of oak, and by 22.8% for one built of fir, according to figures calculated by George Moorsom in 1852. The great drawback to iron hulls was the lack of success in checking the growth of weed and barnacles below the water. Peacock & Buchan's pink-coloured anti-fouling paint, introduced in 1848, gave the best results. It cost about £70 to dock, scrape off the growth and paint-on a composition on the bottom of a 900 ton ship.

Storm Cloud's fastest passage was one of 71 days from the Clyde to Launceston in 1855, Cape Otway being sighted only 66 days out. Her biggest day's run was 370 miles. Otherwise her passages were not out of the ordinary. Stephen's tried in vain to sell her, year after year, and finally succeeded in 1862, but she was wrecked the following year.

Other clippers built by Alexander Stephen & Sons at their Glasgow yard consisted of

This fine example of a lithograph by Thomas G. Dutton evokes the clipper ship era with this portrayal of the barque Spirit of the Age. *Of 737 tons, she was built at Sunderland in 1854 by John Pile.* (Author).

the *Typhoon, Hurricane*, and *John Bell*. Both the last two had ratios of more than 7 beams to length, and the design of *Hurricane* was very similar to another iron ship built in 1853 on the Clyde, the *Lord of the Isles*. This extreme clipper of 691 tons was built at Greenock by Scott & Co for Martin & Co of the same town. On her maiden passage, she was 74 days between the Tuskar Light off the mouth of the Clyde and Sydney harbour, and a passenger claimed that she once ran 428 miles in 24 hours. Although not substantiated by official logbook extracts the letter had a ring of authenticity about it, and if true, this would easily be the longest day's run ever performed by a British-built ship. Runs of over 400 miles are usually ascribed only to American-built ships.

Other iron clippers built on the Clyde included *Gauntlet* (1853 of 693 tons) 'a yacht of large tonnage', *Glen Roy* (1854 of 1,219 tons), *Cairnsmore* (1855 of 1,086 tons) and *Tempest* (1855 of 845 tons).

Another yard building iron clippers was that of Charles Tayleur & Co of Warrington, on the River Mersey. Here the large *Tayleur* of 1,750 tons n.m. was built in 1853, followed by *Startled Fawn* and *Sarah Palmer*, both built in 1855. *Tayleur* had the misfortune to be wrecked on the Irish coast just two days after leaving Liverpool on her maiden passage for Australia; 300 people were drowned. The compasses had not been adjusted. A lines plan and sail plan of *Sarah Palmer* appear in *Fast Sailing Ships*: she did not have much deadrise but her waterlines were fine. Compared with some clippers, the sail plan makes her look under-canvassed. The iron lower masts were naturally hollow but a newspaper reported that they were 'filled with what is technically called "feathers"'. The meaning of this term remains unsolved. The naval architect, John Grantham (1809–74) supervised ships building in this yard, so he may have had a hand in the design.

The clippers had deck layouts no different from other sailing ships and owing to the

Built expressly to compete in the Australian gold rush, the Crest of the Wave *made a maiden passage of 73 days between Liverpool and Melbourne, in 1854. Built the previous year at Sunderland by William Pile, she was of 856 tons.* (Parker Gallery).

sizeable crews still obtainable at cheap rates, not many attempts were made at easing the labour on board. However, Cunningham's topsails which could be controlled from the deck and rolled round the yard when they had to be reefed, presumably saved men going aloft to reef the sails by hand; this roller-reefing device appeared in 1850 and was usually employed in topsails only, but a few ships had it fitted to every square sail. Wire standing rigging was in fairly general use in the 1850s, which reduced the need to continually adjust the slackening and tightening of hemp rigging. As regards the matter of anchor work, better geared windlasses were made by Emerson & Walker and Brown & Harfield. Every ship had a splendid figurehead and there was a long trail board with richly gilded carving supporting the maiden, storm god, or other fanciful creation. There was probably further carving around the stern, and also across the break of the poop. The mouldings and pilasters were almost always in the classical manner, but a few ships, such as the *Spindrift* (1867), used the Gothic style.

Apart from some of the clippers built at Aberdeen and elsewhere which were painted green, black was the most popular colour for the outside of the hulls, only a few ships being painted white. In any case, a black hull with brass-rimmed portholes, and gilded strake and carved work was remarkably handsome. Timber masts were often varnished with black doublings, and the yards were often painted black; another combination was white lower masts, bowsprit and yards with varnished masts: iron masts might be painted pink or yellow ochre, and sometimes combinations of white and black were favoured. Prior to about 1850, deck fittings were often painted the same

The City of Nankin *at the fitting-out berth at Barclay, Curle & Co's yard at Glasgow, shortly after her launch in 1859. Of 986 tons, she was 212 ft long, was built of iron with a square stern, and had fine lines but little deadrise. She was in the India trade. The main yard has not yet been crossed, nor have the royal yards.* (D. W. McDonald).

colour as the inside of the bulwarks, such as blue or green, but the smarter ships began to have the deck fittings finished in varnished wood. Carved work was cheap in those days and itinerant carvers would complete animals' heads or supporters for a coat of arms in a few hours.

Clipper ships were certainly not built regardless of cost, because the owners had invested money in them and had to obtain a return on the capital. In the fifties, Alexander Hall charged from £14 to £18 per ton for wooden clippers, depending on the sort of classification which Lloyd's Register would assign. During the early years of the Australian gold rush, there was so great a demand for ships to take goods out to the gold fields that clippers could obtain a freight of £6 per ton; if they then crossed over to China and loaded a homeward cargo of tea at £5 per ton, they might clear the initial cost of the ship in one or two voyages. Extreme clippers which could carry only a little more than their own register tonnage were good money-spinners under boom conditions, but after the end of the Crimean War, when there was a glut of ships on the market and all freight rates plunged down, life was not so rosy for them. Instead, medium clippers, which could carry twice their register tonnage were the sort of craft that earned their keep.

Other leading builders of clipper ships were the brothers John and William Pile: John, the elder, built at Sunderland until 1854 when he moved to West Hartlepool, but William remained at Sunderland until his death in 1874. John Pile built the three clippers *Spirit of the North* (1853), *Flying Dragon* (1853) and *Spirit of the Age* (1854).

The two *Spirits* were in the China trade, owned by T. A. Gibb of London, and the other was in the Australian trade. The first lithograph by T. G. Dutton which I ever owned was of *Spirit of the Age* and so she has always been a favourite of mine. All three were considered to be large for a barque rig at that time, being over 650 tons, as many full-rigged ships were under 400 tons. John Pile also built the ship *Norna* (1851), the brig *Lizzie Webber* (1852) and the *Mirage* (1855).

Clippers by William Pile included the *Crest of the Wave* (1853), *Spray of the Ocean* (1854), *Kelso* (1855) and *Lammermuir* (1856). The first of these had a coefficient of under-deck tonnage of .55 which is identical to *Cutty Sark* and suggests a sharp-bodied hull. She raced out to Melbourne in 73 days from Liverpool in 1854.

The number of clippers of over 500 tons being built in southern and south-western England was minimal and was principally confined to yards on the River Thames, although the *Sarah Neumann* of 1,004 tons was built at Bideford in 1855 by George Cox and the *Speedy* of 1,031 tons was built at Bridport by Cox & Son—said to be unrelated. Newspapers, eulogizing the launch of a clipper, were fond of saying that she was designed 'on lines said to be unsurpassed by any vessel afloat', but such comments are not worth serious consideration today.

Some clippers were built on the River Thames in the fifties by Thomas Bilbe & Co of Rotherhithe such as the 'long, sharp flush-decked' *Celestial* (1851 of 438 tons n.m.); *Orient* (1853 of 1,032 tons n.m.); *Red Riding Hood* (1857 of 709 tons); and *Lauderdale* (1858 of 851 tons). *Red Riding Hood* was their first ship built on composite construction with an iron frame and wood planking; she was broken up in 1890. Another clipper built on the Thames was the *Northfleet* which Thomas Pitcher built in 1853 of 951 tons n.m. She is partly remembered for her tragic end when the Spanish steamer *Murillo* ran her down in 1873 off Dungeness, where she sank with the loss of 293 lives. But she is also remembered for three fine outward passages to Hong Kong: 94 days in 1856, 88 days from Start Point in 1857, and 89 days from Start Point in 1858.

At one time it was believed that the design of the British clipper *Challenger* was based on that of the American clipper *Oriental*, whose lines were taken off early in 1851 by the Lloyd's Register surveyors Waymouth and Cornish. A comparison of the plans of the two ships show unmistakable differences proving that the British ship was built without American influence. The whole subject was discussed in greater detail in my earlier book, *The China Bird*.

The story goes that at a City dinner in 1851, the shipbuilder, Richard Green, made a speech in which he attempted to rouse the spirit of British shipowners and urged them to challenge American competition. As a result of this, the clipper *Challenger* of 699 tons is said to have been born. She was built by R. & H. Green at the Blackwall Yard. The big American clipper *Challenge* of 2,006 tons was lauched on 24th May 1851 while the British ship was still under construction. The American Navigation Club's challenge for an American clipper to race a British one from England to China and back for a stake of £10,000, was not issued until September 1852, and so was not the reason for building the *Challenger*. The race was never sailed. But the two clippers had already raced each other home in 1852 between the following ports:

Challenger (Capt Killick)	Shanghai to London, 18 July to 17 Nov. 1852, 112 days off Anjer 14 Sept.
Challenge (Capt Pitts)	Canton to Gravesend, 5 Aug to 19 Nov, 1852, 106 days off Anjer 12 Sept; arrived Deal 18 Nov.

A typical painting done in the Western manner by a Chinese artist depicts the Caduceus *approaching Hong Kong under full sail with skysails set. She was built on the River Thames by Fletcher in 1854 and was of 1116 tons. In 1855–56 she sailed out to Sydney in 84 days and came home from Whampoa in 125 days.* (Parker Gallery).

It must be remembered that Shanghai is some 850 miles dead to leeward of Canton at the time of the south-west monsoon, so the *Challenge*'s six days shorter on overall time was nothing to boast about. In addition, it will be seen that Killick in *Challenger* was four days quicker on the passage from Anjer to London which was good going: he took only 64 days on this leg.

Under Killick, the *Challenger*'s first nine homeward passages were all made between Shanghai or Hankow and London, the average being 115 days; when tea was loaded at Hankow, the departure date is calculated from passing Woosung. After Killick left in 1860, the average for the next eight passages between the same points rises to 129 days. James Killick gave up the sea in 1860 and the next year was joined by James Martin to found the Firm of Killick & Martin; the name was altered to Killick, Martin & Co in 1863 when David Ritchie became a partner, and the firm is still flourishing.

But in 1853 *Challenger* and the American clipper *Nightingale* both set sail from Shanghai on 8 August, and the British ship got to Deal two days ahead or 110 days later, which was a smart performance.

Whereas in the 1860s there were a dozen or more passages made from China to ports in England that took less than 100 days when the time of departure was made during the prevalence of the south-west monsoon in the China Sea—May to end of

September—there appear to be only three passages under 100 days that were made at the same time of the year during the 1850s. These were as follows:

1856 *Spirit of the Age* (Capt W. Billing)	Whampoa to Deal, 21 Aug to 28 Nov, 99 days, passed Anjer 13 Sept
1857 *Fiery Cross* (Capt J. Dallas)	Foochow to London, 9 Aug to 16 Nov, 99 days, passed Anjer 29 Aug; passed Dartmouth 94 days out
1858 *Robin Hood* (Capt G. Cobb)	Foochow to London, 9 Sept to 17 Dec, 99 days, passed Anjer 7 Oct

(The above times are from *The Tea Clippers*).

It was considered the acme of a passage from China to perform it in under 100 days *against* the monsoon, which necessitated a beat to windward down the dangerous and poorly charted China Sea, and tested the nerves of the master and the abilities of the ship to the utmost.

Of the above three ships, *Fiery Cross* has so far not been mentioned. She was designed by the naval architect William Rennie and built by Rennie, Johnson & Rankine at Liverpool in 1855 of 672 tons with dimensions of 174 ft (keel and forerake) × 30 ft × 19 ft. Her hull-form was somewhat after *Challenger*'s but there was more hollow in the waterlines at bow and stern, and she had a heavy square stern and full height poop which broke the line of the sheer. Nevertheless, the Melbourne newspapers termed her a 'smart and race-horsey looking ship' when she arrived there on her maiden passage in December 1855, 81 days out from Liverpool, with 1,200 tons of cargo. In 1856, the first ship to reach London with the new season's tea received a premium of £1 per ton, and this further stimulated the races. In 1857, *Fiery Cross* loaded at £6. 6s per ton at Foochow, which was a high rate.

William Rennie, who was 'celebrated as the finest marine draughtsman in England', was responsible for the designs of such clippers as *Gauntlet*, *Fiery Cross* (1855), *Fiery Cross* (1860), *Black Prince*, *John R. Worcester*, *Norman Court* and the auxiliary steamer *Sea King*.

In north-west England, shipbuilders at Workington such as Charles Lamport and the Workington & Harrington Shipbuilding Co were building clippers for Eastern trades such as *Cambalu* (1852), *Aerolite* (1853), *Banian* (1856), *Jubilee* (1857), *Scawfell* (1858) and *Dunmail* (1859). A painting of the latter shows her setting a main moonsail above the skysail. *Scawfell* made a record run from Macao to Point Lynas, near Liverpool, of only 85 days early in 1861.

On the River Clyde, Robert Steele & Co launched their first tea clipper, the *Kate Carnie*, in 1855, followed by *Ellen Rodger* (1858) and *Falcon* (1859). A lines plan of the *Falcon* (plate IV in *The Tea Clippers*), indicates that her hull-form was somewhat similar to the clippers *Ariel* and *Sir Lancelot* which Steele built six years later; the chief difference was in size, *Falcon* being six feet shorter and 18 inches narrower. Captain Keay who commanded both *Falcon* and *Ariel* said that the latter was a knot faster all round. Phillips, Shaw & Lowther of London later to become Shaw, Lowther & Maxton, owned *Falcon*, *Ariel* and *Titania*. A recently discovered spar and standing rigging plan of *Falcon* shows that she carried trysail gaffs on both fore and main masts.

In the Australian trade, the fastest ships mostly sailed between Liverpool and Melbourne, and many of the ships involved had been built in America or Canada. They sailed under such flags as the Black Ball Line, owned by James Baines & Co; the White Star Line, owned by Pilkington & Wilson; the Golden Line, owned by Miller &

The barque Teazer *has the appearance of being a clipper, with her raking stem. She has been identified as being built at Dartmouth by Kelly in 1858 and registering 293 tons net. She made a passage to Durban of 55 days from London in about 1874 under the command of Captain Storm. In* Fast Sailing Ships *fig 227, I assigned the above particulars to a brig of the same name (also reproduced here on page 95), as* Lloyd's Register *allots her a brig rig between 1868-71. The 1872 edition of* American Lloyd's *allots her rig as barque when seen in June 1871 and states that she belongs to the port of Kingston, Jamaica. It appears that Captain Storm became her owner in 1872 and the ship was registered in Jamaica. Either there is a discrepancy in the rig entries or else two different vessels with somewhat similar hulls are involved. The rake of the stem is similar in each case, but the brig's stern has a topgallant rail around it; also the barque probably has a raised quarter deck, whereas the brig has a flush deck. (Local History Museum, Durban).*

Thompson; and James Beazley. Many of the Black Ball Line ships were built in Canada such as *Marco Polo, Indian Queen, Oliver Laing, Morning Light* and so on; they were all big ships of over 1,500 tons. In short-cutting the time between England and Australia with her passage of 68 days to Melbourne in 1852, the *Marco Polo* founded the fortunes of James Baines. He chartered many vessels, such as McKay's big clipper *Sovereign of the Seas,* and then proceeded to order four ships from Donald McKay of Boston: the extreme clippers *Lightning* and *James Baines,* the clipper *Champion of the Seas,* and the medium clipper *Donald McKay.* In 1860 his star was at its zenith because in that year, according to Basil Lubbock, he owned 86 ships and employed 3,300 officers and men.

Although many American and Canadian-built ships were owned in Great Britain, they are described in Chapter Five which deals with ships built in North America.

Ships sailing from Liverpool to Melbourne averaged $110\frac{1}{2}$ days in 1852 and $105\frac{1}{2}$ days in 1853; whereas, ships sailing from London averaged 123 and 126 days in the respective years. Lieutenant Matthew F. Maury, who was collecting data from log-books to recommend sailing directions, addressed the members of Lloyds' in the summer of 1853, and reminded them that he had predicted the previous Spring that the passage times between the United Kingdom or America to Australia could be cut to 70 or 75 days both ways; now the *Marco Polo* had proved he was right. He inferred that his sailing directions were much better than those issued by the Admiralty. By degrees, shipmasters began to learn what course to take at a particular season of the year in order to find the best wind for the next leg of their voyage, but it was a hard process to convince all of them.

There were never many passages made either to or from Australia in less than 70 days, and anything less than 75 days was considered to be fast. In 1853, when the urge to get to the goldfields was beginning to reach fever heat, some ships were taking five months on the passage, and several of the steam-assisted ships were very slow. The problem which most shipmasters faced when reaching Melbourne was that of preventing their entire crew deserting to go up-country to the gold regions. Captain Forbes of the *Marco Polo* had his crew locked up by the police in 1852, after the gold nuggets thrown aboard by visitors had made them unruly; and they remained in confinement until the ship was ready to sail, when they were brought aboard after the ship was actually under way. Their visit to the Colony was therefore of short duration.

[**Right**] *Pictured bows-on in dry-dock is the* Oronsay *which was built in 1859 under the name of* Slieve Donard. *Probably a medium clipper, she was built of iron at Liverpool by Vernon of 1,499 tons for the India trade. The lines of the iron plating can be seen and also the decoration of painted ports.* (National Maritime Museum).

[**Opposite**] *The* Star of Peace, *built at Aberdeen in 1855 of 1113 tons, was probably only a medium clipper. She is here seen at Sydney in the 1860's lying at Circular Quay where many ships were photographed. She has Cunningham's roller-reefing topsails with the tell-tale roller mechanism at the centre of each yard. The rigging on this photograph has been strengthened, not always too successfully, and the tears and blemishes on the edges have been painted out.* (D. M. Little).

CHAPTER FIVE

American Clippers of the 1850's

Although British and American clippers were compared side by side in Chapter Three it seems easier to tell their story in separate chapters after 1850, as not only the ships themselves but their construction and the trades for which they were built differed so markedly. Clippers built in America or Canada for British owners are also described in this chapter where it is appropriate.

Considering that gold was first found on 24 January 1848 at Sutter's Mill on the Sacramento River in California, it took a surprisingly long time for the first large clipper ships to be launched. Within two years of the discovery, a quarter of a million people flocked to the goldfields from the far distant quarters of the world, and all had to arrive by sea as the journey across the United States had not yet been opened. Of course, confirmation of such news always takes time to be absorbed and it was really only in the autumn of 1848 that the newspapers on the eastern seaboard of America were stating in unequivocal terms that there really was enough gold for everyone. So the rush was on, and the 'Forty-Niners' made their trip out there in 1849. In the twelve months up to 1 April 1848, only four merchant vessels and nine whalers called at San Francisco; in 1849, 775 vessels cleared from Atlantic ports to the land of gold. What a remarkable contrast!

The *Sea Queen* left New York in December 1848 and reached San Francisco in 125 days under Captain G. F. Manson, possibly the fastest passage yet made out around the Horn. Most vessels took 150 to 250 days. During 1849, some clippers made the passage out, such as the 1,000-ton *Memnon* which took 123 days, but shipowners were still content with only moderately fast ships that could carry a large cargo. But in the course of 1849, orders were finally placed for ships of larger size and finer lines than had ever been built before.

At that time there were three basic types of hull-form for clippers: one was developed from the Baltimore clipper with steep deadrise and fine ends; another was the packet model having a full midship section and little deadrise but long sharp waterlines; a third was a compromise between the two. On the whole, William Webb favoured the development of the packet model, whereas Donald McKay varied between the steep-floored *Stag Hound* and the full midship section of *James Baines*.

Meanwhile the voyage time to San Francisco was being rapidly shortened. First there was the 109 day passage of *Samuel Russell*, which was diverted from the China trade. She arrived in May 1850. Two months later another China trader, the *Sea Witch*, sailed through the Golden Gate only 97 days at sea from New York, having rounded

One of the products of the California gold rush—abandoned and waiting ships, photographed here in San Francisco Bay in the winter of 1852-53. Some are trying to obtain crews; others have been left to rot. (Smithsonian Institution).

the Horn in mid-winter. These two ships were smaller and therefore less powerful than the clippers about to be launched.

The first clipper of any size built specifically for the California trade appears to be the *Celestial* of 860 tons, built by William Webb, and launched on 9 June 1850 at his yard in New York. She was broad in the beam with moderate deadrise, a short entrance but a longer run, yet not so fine-lined as either *Sea Witch* (1846) or *Samuel Russell* (1847). Her maiden passage to San Francisco occupied 104 days.

Also nearing completion in New York were two much larger ships—the *Eclipse* of 1,223 tons built by Jabez Williams and the *White Squall* of 1,119 tons by Jacob Bell. The latter's cost, including provisions and stores for one year, was $90,000, and yet her freight on her maiden passage was no less than $70,000. She would therefore entirely clear her first cost on the complete voyage. No wonder there was such a rush to order and construct clippers.

The first large clipper to be built outside New York was the *Surprise* of 1,261 tons; her design is credited to Samuel Pook, and she was launched from Samuel Hall's yard at East Boston. She went down the ways fully-rigged with her three skysail yards crossed, which much delighted the spectators. Pook is said to have also designed the medium clipper *Gamecock* as well as the *Witchcraft*, both built in 1850. The *Surprise* was a very handsome and profitable ship. Her first master was Philip Dumaresq, one of the best known clipper captains, and he took the ship out to San Francisco in the fast time of 96 days 15 hours.

The first clipper built by George Raynes was the *Sea Serpent*, launched in November 1850 in Portsmouth, New Hampshire, with dimensions of 196.9 ft × 39.2 ft × 20.8 ft and 1,402 tons; she had steep deadrise. Her owners were Grinnell, Minturn & Co of New York, and she was the pioneer ship of their Californian Line. The Journal of a voyage made in her to California and China in 1854–55 was published by the Mariners' Museum in 1975.

The last big clipper to be launched in 1850 was the *Stag Hound* which came from Donald McKay's yard at East Boston. It was a cold winter with deep snow on the ground and ice in the harbour, and it was feared the tallow would freeze on the launching ways. So just prior to her launch, boiling whale oil was poured over the ways, and when the shores were knocked away, she glided quickly into the icy waters. Captain Arthur Clark recounts how she was christened informally by the yard foreman who, breaking a bottle of Medford rum across her forefoot, shouted out 'Stag Hound, your name's Stag Hound'. Builders were always secretive about their products and were usually loathe to allow even the owners to retain a plan of the lines or a half-model, so it seems surprising to read that Donald McKay actually granted an interview to reporters prior to laying her keel in August 1850, even telling them he was going to build a ship of 1,200 tons about 185 feet long. Rival shipowners ordered vessels of twelve to thirteen hundred tons. Stag Hound was constructed in only four months, and when she took to the water on 7 December, it was found that her actual size was 1,534 tons with dimensions of 215 ft × 39.8 ft × 21 ft; so the business rivals had been clearly hoodwinked in no uncertain manner.

The Stag Hound was McKay's first clipper. She had considerable deadrise with a deep keel; a very long entrance and run without any hollows in the waterlines; very little tumblehome; a round stern; but a plain bow in which the bowsprit entered the hull quite abruptly without any trailboards or head knee. She had a short poop and forecastle, and a long open main deck with high bulwarks; abaft the foremast was a big deckhouse. Aloft, she crossed three skysails and was altogether very heavily rigged. The main yard measured 86 ft and considerably overlapped the fore yard and the crossjack yard. But only six days after setting sail for San Francisco, the main topmast broke off and brought down the three topgallant masts. This was only the first of many partial dismastings suffered by the hard-driven Californian clippers. They rarely put back, but fashioned new spars on board and re-rigged them, perhaps putting into Rio or Valparaiso for additional repairs.

Stag Hound's maiden voyage took her to San Francisco, Manilla, Whampoa and home with tea to New York. The profits made in 10 months and 23 days enabled the original cost of the ship to be paid off and still leave $80,000 to be divided among Sampson & Tappan, her owners.

While Stag Hound was under construction, William Webb announced in October that he intended to begin work on an even larger clipper. This was the Challenge, built to the order of Griswold & Co of New York. At the end of 1850, Webb had three other clippers under construction, the Comet, Invincible and the steep-floored Gazelle. Other yards were equally busy as shipowners were now in a great hurry to get fast sailing ships quickly into the water in order to reap the benefits of the booming trade with California and secure the largest possible profit for themselves. 'Measurement goods' commanded a freight of $1 per cubic foot, and $60 to $70 per ton was charged for bulkier cargoes. At Boston, McKay had begun work on the Flying Cloud.

The height of clipper ship building in America occurred in the three years 1851–1853, after which the only extreme clippers were the Lightning and Sunny South, launched in 1854. The peak years of clipper building in Britain were a year or two behind these, because the development of the tea trade from China and the gold discovery in Australia did not find a response from the shipowners until late in 1852.

When comparing the years of clipper ship building in the two countries, it is worth reiterating the point that tonnage in America was, until 1865, measured by the old manner which had been abandoned in Great Britain in 1836. This 'old measurement' tonnage assumed that depth was half the breadth and the tonnage was calculated by the simple formula $[(L - \frac{3}{5}B) \times B \times \frac{1}{2}B] \div 95$, where L is the length on the deck from the fore part of the stem below the bowsprit to the after part of the sternpost above the upper deck, and B is the maximum breadth outside above the main wales. (In vessels with only one deck, the depth of hold had to be measured.) The resultant figure gives an inflated size relative to the tonnage of British clippers, as shown below:

Ship	Tons by 'old measurement'	'New tons' in America after 1864	Tons in UK after 1854
Challenge	2,006	1,375	—
Witch of the Wave	1,498	975	—
Champion of the Seas	2,447	—	1,947 (gross)
Flying Cloud	1,782	—	1,139
Great Republic (as rebuilt)	3,356	2,751	—
Cairngorm	1,246	—	939
Eastern Monarch	1,849	—	1,631
Robin Hood	1,185	—	853

All eyes were focused on the clippers *Flying Cloud* and *Challenge* in May 1851: the

Seen at anchor in the River Thames with a spritsail barge alongside, the Storm King *was built at Chelsea, Massachusetts, in 1853 of 1148 tons.* (National Maritime Museum).

former was loading at New York at the start of what was to be a record breaking run; the other was almost ready for launching. Both ships were the result of fiercely individual designers' ideas and their hull-forms were quite different. The McKay clipper had moderate deadrise, little tumblehome, a raking stem, long fine ends with the maximum beam placed amidships, and with slight hollows in the waterlines near bow and stern. Webb's clipper, *Challenge*—the most extreme clipper he ever built—had greater deadrise with sides rounding up all the way and marked tumblehome, a more vertical stem, the maximum beam placed much further forward so that the run was much longer than the entrance, although the load waterline was not so sharp as in *Flying Cloud*; hollows in entrance and run were also much more exaggerated than in *Flying Cloud*. The latter measured 229.0 ft × 40.8 ft × 21.6 ft and 1,782 tons (under later British ownership the tonnage was 1,139). The *Challenge* measured 230.6 ft × 43.2 ft × 26.0 ft and 2,006 tons. Both ships were heavily sparred and rigged, but Webb's clipper carried masts and yards of immense length for her size. The total length of mainmast from heel to truck was $210\frac{1}{2}$ ft, length of main yard 90 ft, distance between the outer leaches of the square lower stunsails on the foremast was 160 ft. These huge sizes were because her first master, Robert Waterman, insisted on increasing the sail area beyond what Webb had designed, and subsequently her spars were shortened on at least two occasions.

Ships of such extreme proportions needed captains of remarkable qualities as well as competent crews: both the above clippers had the best commanders that could be found, but whereas Captain Josiah Cressy in the *Flying Cloud* had a good crew, Robert Waterman in *Challenge* had a tough mutinous crowd who were only interested in getting to the diggings.

July was a bad month to sail in and the light winds met by *Challenge* delayed her passage to 108 days which greatly disappointed her admirers. But the rotten crew also hindered the clipper as only six of them could steer, and the others caused many ugly scenes so that the officers never went on deck unless they were armed. By the time of her arrival at San Francisco, five of the crew had died from disease, four had been drowned after falling from aloft, and two had been killed by the captain when defending his mate from being murdered. The Vigilant Committee had to protect Waterman and eventually dispersed the mob who clamoured for his death; at a trial his reputation was cleared. Undoubtedly he was a hard man to sail under, but 'over-hatted' clippers brought out both the best and worst in everyone.

After various cross-Pacific passages, the *Challenge* finally sailed from Whampoa in August 1852 with a cargo of tea for London, making the passage in 105 days to Deal. Her so-called race with the British *Challenger* was told in the previous chapter. *Challenge* was renamed *Golden City* in 1861 when sold; in 1866 she was bought by Wilson & Co of South Shields and was lost in 1876.

The *Flying Cloud*'s maiden passage was celebrated for its brevity: it only lasted 89 days and 21 hours from 2 June to 21 August 1851. Her logbook records the frequent loss of spars and their replacement, the splitting of sails, the strong winds which drove the ship at over 18 knots, and the maximum day's run of 374 miles—quite the longest distance then run in 24 hours. This splendid passage has only twice been beaten and that by only a few hours in each case. In 1859 the *Andrew Jackson* took 89 days 4 hours; in 1854, *Flying Cloud* herself was only 89 days 8 hours on the run. The partisans for *Andrew Jackson* versus *Flying Cloud* are firmly convinced that their ship made the shorter passage.

The lofty clipper Challenge *was built on extremely fine lines by Wiliam Webb in 1851. In this lithograph, the artist has obviously drawn the eagle figurehead too large.* (Author).

But there was a whole host of other clippers built in 1851. At New York, William H. Webb built the *Swordfish, Comet, Gazelle,* and *Invincible*—a large output for a single year. With a length on deck of 170 ft, *Swordfish* was smaller than the others but her maiden passage of 91 days to San Francisco was the fourth fastest ever made there. The *Comet* was a fast and successful clipper, 228 ft long on deck and carrying three skysails, but was not over-sparred. Like many American ships of this date, she carried standing trysail gaffs on both fore and main masts. She had many record passages to her credit such as the record from San Francisco to New York of 76 days made in 1853–54 under Captain Gardner; also a record passage from Liverpool to Hong Kong in 1854 of 83 days 21 hours pilot to pilot, or 86 days 16 hours anchorage to anchorage. The *Gazelle* had the greatest deadrise of all Webb's clippers, but he claimed no merit for this, saying it was an owner's requirement which reduced her power to carry sail. In all Webb's designs, the entrance was short and sharp, and the run long and tapered.

Another clipper with steep deadrise which appeared in 1851 was the *Nightingale*, built at Portsmouth, New Hampshire, by Samuel Hanscom Jnr to transport Americans to the Great Exhibition of 1851. However, this fell through, and she was diverted to the tea trade between China and England. In 1860 she became a slaver.

Another shipbuilder at Portsmouth was George Raynes who built the medium clipper *Wild Pigeon* and the clipper *Witch of the Wave* in 1851. The latter had a cross-section at maximum beam somewhat similar to Webb's *Challenge* with marked deadrise and sides that rounded up all the way to the rail; but her ends were more evenly balanced and the waterlines were not of such extreme sharpness as in Webb's ship. Her dimensions were 204 ft 0 in (between perpendiculars) × 39 ft 8 in (moulded) × 21 ft 0 in and 1,498 tons; her owners were Glidden & Williams of Salem. She was sold to Dutch owners in 1857 and renamed *Electra*; the Bureau Veritas Register of 1871 gives her tonnage as 1,117. Her maiden passage occupied 123 days to San Francisco which was 18 days longer than expected, but she then crossed over to Hong Kong in 40 days and, sailing for London on 5th January 1852 from Whampoa, took her pilot off Dungeness 90 days later, which was a fast passage.

The *Typhoon* was also built at Portsmouth, New Hampshire, and was launched with her skysail yards crossed. Her owners sent her across to Liverpool in March 1851; she was only 11½ days to Cape Clear and 13½ days port to port. She excited much interest on arrival, being one of the earliest American clippers of large size seen there.

At Boston, Donald McKay built the extreme clipper *Flying Fish* in 1851 which proved very fast in the California trade, the average of seven passages around the Horn being only 105⁴⁄₇ days. On her second voyage she took only 92 days to San Francisco. She had much less deadrise than *Stag Hound* but was more hollow in the waterlines. McKay also built the *Staffordshire* as a trans-Atlantic packet, but on clipper lines.

Other notable clippers launched in 1851 were the *N. B. Palmer*, built at New York by Westervelt & MacKay of 1,399 tons for A. A. Low & Bros; the *Hurricane* built at Hoboken, New York, which had Cunningham's roller-reefing topsails; the *Seaman's Bride*, built at Baltimore of 668 tons, which carried a moonsail on each mast above her skysails, a most unusual rig.

The clippers of 1851 which returned to their home ports during 1852 fresh from their triumphs and struggles against wind and wave had much damage aloft to get repaired. Many masts were sprung and fished, spars were lashed together, topmast fids crushed, and rigging sadly in need of replacement. These clippers were so much larger in size than any previous vessels built on fine lines and they had been subjected to much more abuse by the hard driving around Cape Horn. The builders, riggers and sail makers had had no experience to fall back on when sizing the spars and rigging needed for the ships as they lay at the fitting-out berths before they sailed. Now they were remasted with stouter spars and stronger rigging to face the exigences of the next round of passages across the globe. Much valuable experience had been gained, and not least of all by the masters and officers. Twenty years later, British shipbuilders faced just such a crisis as their latest iron clippers of much enlarged tonnage and increased sail area were being dismasted on the Australian run, following the opening of the Suez Canal.

Gold was discovered in Australia in May 1851, and soon Sydney and Melbourne were repeating the scenes witnessed in San Francisco as prospectors arrived in ship after ship, and large clippers were in demand to race to the eastward in the southern hemisphere before the 'Roaring Forties', as the winds were called. The *Nightingale* cleared for Melbourne in October 1851 and other clippers followed her. This was a great tonic for shipbuilders in Canada who were not slow to commence building big wooden ships on finer lines, and send them across the Atlantic to tempt prospective buyers in Liverpool. With clippers available in America, the Australian gold rush was more quickly supplied with big, fast ships than was the case with California.

By far the most celebrated American clipper built in 1852 was the *Sovereign of the Seas*, built by Donald McKay. She was a large ship, even by American standards, measuring 258 ft 2 in × 44 ft 7 in × 23 ft 6 in and 2,420 tons. Developing the hull-form from his clipper *Flying Fish*, McKay gave her less deadrise and less tumblehome, but more sheer and decidedly finer waterlines. The entrance was long and hollow, and the

This dramatic photograph shows the Syren *at New Bedford with her sails clewed up and drying. She was a medium clipper, built in 1851 by John Taylor at Medford, Mass., and of 1064 tons o.m. She was still in service in 1920 under the name of* Margarida *of Buenos Ayres.* (Peabody Museum of Salem).

run was long but a little less hollow. Her figurehead was a sea god, half fish, half man; the stem was plain as in many American clippers, without any trail boards although some carving ran up to the figurehead. Donald McKay built her on speculation and so she embodied his ideas of what a clipper should be, untramelled by the whims of a shipowner. The New York brokers Funch & Meinke bought her and resold her to Hamburg owners in 1854. She had a main yard 90 ft long but only carried a skysail on the mainmast. In the words of Arthur H. Clark she 'combined grace and beauty with immense strength and power to carry sail.'

Although her maiden passage to San Francisco took 103 days she sailed in the unfavourable month of August and therefore it was considered excellent. She had a crew totalling 105 with Lauchlan McKay—younger brother of Donald McKay—in command. From San Francisco she went to Honolulu and there loaded a cargo of sperm oil for New York, the passage taking her south-eastwards across the Pacific and back around Cape Horn. This last leg of the voyage was covered in the remarkably short time of 82 days, or from 13 February to 6 May 1853. She was only able to ship a crew of 34 men before the mast and also had the misfortune to spring her fore topmast. Nevertheless, she averaged 378 miles for four consecutive days on one occasion and on another averaged 330 miles for eleven consecutive days. Her greatest noon to noon run was of 411 miles on 18 March, during which the log records a speed of 19 knots for three successive hours.

On her next passage, Donald McKay accompanied his brother. This took the clipper to Liverpool in 13 days 23 hours dock to dock, 18 June to 2 July 1853, but only 6 days from Cape Race, Newfoundland, to Cape Clear, Ireland. This was the first time the New York to Liverpool run had been completed in less than 14 days. No wonder that Donald McKay was now considered the clipper ship builder *par excellence*. Carl Cutler sums up her performances, in *Greyhounds of the Sea*, in these words: 'It seems doubtful indeed whether the ship was ever built that could pass the *Sovereign of the Seas* under proper trim in strong plain sail breezes, with Lauchlan McKay in command'.

Under the command of Warner, previously her first mate, she went out to Melbourne in 78 days and returned to Liverpool in only 68 days. During her first voyage for her new German owners in 1854, when bound to Sydney, she claimed a speed of 22 knots.

Another clipper built on speculation in 1852 was the *Jacob Bell*, built in New York by the shipbuilder after whom the ship was named; she was bought by A. A. Low & Bros in 1856 and kept in Eastern trades.

Samuel Pook designed the ships *Defiance*, which was built by George Thomas at Rockland, and *Golden West*, built by Paul Curtis at East Boston. Other ships built this year by Curtis included *Golden Fleece* and *Queen of the Seas*—all names designed to stir the imagination. George Raynes built the *Tinqua* of 668 tons, which was small by current standards. At East Boston, Donald McKay built the *Bald Eagle* of 1,703 tons and the *Westward Ho* of 1,650 tons.

In Liverpool, James Baines had acquired the deep-hulled *Marco Polo* in the early part of 1852 and fitted her out for the booming Australia trade. She had been built at St John, New Brunswick, Canada, in 1851, by James Smith and measured 184.1 ft × 36.3 ft × 29.4 ft, 1,400 tons o.m. and 1,625 tons n.m. A lines plan in *Fast Sailing Ships*, Figure 195, shows that she was almost flat-bottomed, and that although the lower part of the entrance and run were sharp and hollow, the load line was quite full. She was six feet deeper than a normal ship, but this gave her enormous capacity

The Marco Polo *firing a gun to announce her arrival, possibly on the return from her record breaking maiden voyage. She is signalling her name, using Marryat's code flags on the mizen. Her main topsail is shaking as it is being clewed up. She was built in 1851 at St John, N.B., and measured 1625 tons n.m.* (New Brunswick Museum).

and immense power to stand heavy driving and sail carrying. In fact, Captain James N. Forbes drove the ship relentlessly on her maiden voyage in 1852 and succeeded in reaching Melbourne in 74 days from Liverpool, 4 July to 16 September, or 68½ days land to land. Melbourne was stunned by this rapid passage and Forbes' reputation was made. Of the 930 Government emigrants which made the trip in her, 51 children and two adults died. Her biggest day's run was 364 miles. She returned to Liverpool in 76 days and in fact actually brought back the news of her arrival out there. This was in the days before submarine cables for telegrams, and her passages were quicker than the scheduled steamers. Captain Forbes had her for another voyage before he was transferred to Baines' new clipper *Lightning*.

Other Canadian ships which were built in 1852 that possibly had clipper pretensions were *Ben Nevis* of 1,347 tons built by Smith at St John; *Miles Barton* of 963 tons built by the Wright Bros at St John; *Indian Queen* of 1,040 tons built at Miramichi; and *Golden Age* of 1,241 tons also built at St John and reputed to have logged 22 knots.

Shipyards were busy throughout the year of 1852 as orders for new clippers flowed in, so that the productions for 1853 included some of the finest and fastest ships yet seen. Samuel Pook designed the *Belle of the West*, *Fearless*, *Herald of the Morning* and the large *Red Jacket*. The latter was built at Rockland, Maine, by George Thomas and measured 251.2 ft × 44.0 ft × 31.0 ft and 2,305 tons. She was an extreme clipper with long sharp ends but with not much deadrise and almost vertical sides. She was launched in November and then was towed to New York to receive her masts and rigging, and was judged a very handsome specimen. She began her historic trans-Atlantic passage in January 1854 and, leaving New York on the 10th, she passed the Bell Buoy 12 days later and anchored at Liverpool in 13 days, 1 hour and 25 minutes. Her average speed was just over 343 miles per day, which really was fast sailing; the greatest day's run was 413 miles. She was chartered by the White Star Line for a voyage to Melbourne and back. The passage was made in 69½ days between Rock Light and Port Philip Heads, and the return trip occupied 73 days. Homeward bound, the clipper encountered extensive ice around Cape Horn and several huge bergs. After this, she stayed in the Australia trade for some years.

William Webb's last extreme clipper, the *Young America*, was built in 1853 for George Daniels of New York. She was an extremely fast, reliable and successful ship and was always popular and admired wherever she went. Of 1,961 tons, she followed Webb's usual hull-form, and in her sail plan a main moonsail is drawn above the main skysail. On the whole, Webb's sail plans tended to be tall and 'narrow' whereas McKay's tended to be 'squarer' with the sails on the mainmast overlapping the others considerably. On the *Young America*'s sail plan, prodigious staysails are drawn between the masts, and there are standing trysail gaffs on fore and main masts. She traded almost exclusively to and from California for thirty years; twenty consecutive passages from New York to San Francisco averaged 117 days.

Two other ships built in 1853 by Webb were the *Flyaway* and the *Snap Dragon*.

At Donald McKay's yard, five splendid ships were launched in this year: the extreme clippers *Great Republic*, *Romance of the Seas* and *Empress of the Seas*; and the clippers *Chariot of Fame* and *Star of Empire*. What names to conjure with! Of course, *Great Republic* requires a book to herself. *Romance of the Seas* was long and narrow for a big American clipper, measuring 240.0 ft × 39.6 ft × 20.0 ft and 1,782 tons. She had six beams to length and was 3½ ft shallower than *Sovereign of the Seas*. She was McKay's last extreme clipper for the California trade. She made several passages from China to England with tea, but none were record-breaking.

The *Great Republic* was built by McKay at his own expense for the Australia trade and was the largest extreme clipper ever built. Superlatives abound when describing her. When launched and completed, she was the largest merchant sailing ship ever built in America, and the first four-masted barque built since the rig appeared on the two 'raft' ships composed of logs—the *Columbus* and *Baron Renfrew*—in the 1820s. Her dimensions were prodigious: 335 ft × 53 ft × 38 ft and 4,555 tons. She had four decks, the upper one being flush, and was launched on 4th October 1853. She was rigged with double topsails on Captain Forbes' plan in which the lower topsail yard hoisted on the topmast *below* the lower mast cap; there were skysails on fore and main only, and the gaff sail on the jigger was comparatively narrow. The main yard was 120 ft, the fore yard 110 ft and the crossjack yard 90 ft. She was towed to New York and loaded with cargo for Liverpool, but tragedy struck on Boxing Day. A great fire broke out in a bakery at midnight and the wind carried the sparks on to the clipper, setting the sails on fire. Soon the masts were ablaze, and the rigging was cut away in an endeavour to save

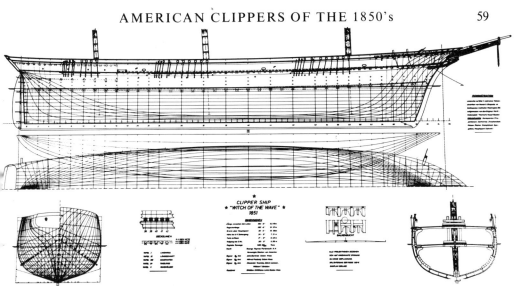

[Above] *Lines plan of the extreme clipper* Witch of the Wave, *built in 1851. She has considerable deadrise with very rounded or 'slack' bilges, and there is very little hollow in her waterlines. Plan drawn by Peter Rückert. (Author).*

[Below] *This model by Donald McNarry represents the* Witch of the Wave *of 1851 and illustrates the ratio between the hull and the lofty masts. (Parker Gallery).*

the hull, but this proved an unwise decision as the falling masts pierced the decks and set the cargo and hull on fire. Although she was scuttled, she burned for two days until flames reached the water's edge. She was then abandoned to the underwriters.

The burning and destruction of this grand ship was a terrible blow to McKay, both financially and mentally.

She was eventually sold to A. A. Low & Bros and rebuilt, to much the same profile as before; her measurements were now 302.2 ft × 48.4 ft × 29.2 ft and 3,356 tons. She was still a huge size although her 'spar' deck was now gone; yet it was said that her hull was as attractive as ever. The masts and yards were greatly reduced in length, and the main yard was now 100 ft long, but she was still rigged as a four-masted barque with double topsails to Howes' patent. On 24 February 1855 she set sail for Liverpool and took 12 days from land to land and 19 days to dock. The next eighteen months were spent chartered as a supply ship in the Crimea, but in December 1856 she sailed from New York to San Francisco which she reached in only 92 days. Numerous voyages followed. In 1869 she was sold to owners in Liverpool and renamed *Denmark*. Three years later she was abandoned at sea.

The *Great Republic* was given a jigger mast so that the braces of the upper yards on the mizen could be led aft. But it was probably in 1862 that the jigger was removed, making her a three-masted full-rigged ship, a rig which she retained for the rest of her life. A survey report of her in 1870 stated that she was 'trussed up with transverse bars of iron screwed up amidships, like an old barn, because the knee fastenings at the end of the deck beams were rotten'.

Of other clippers built in 1853, the *Sweepstakes* was an extreme model, being built by Westervelt at New York for Chambers & Heiser of New York. She was of 1,735 tons and stuck on the launching ways before heeling over on to some adjacent staging. Eventually she was launched and fitted out. She had considerable deadrise and a very sharp entrance and run; she was heavily sparred. On her third voyage she made the eighth fastest time between New York and San Francisco, taking 94 days 19 hours pilot to pilot. This was in 1856. She usually crossed over to load tea in China either for London or New York.

Other celebrated ships built in 1853 included such well-known names as the Atlantic packet *Dreadnought*, the *David Crockett*, *Eagle Wing*, *David Brown*, *Neptune's Car*, *Pride of America*, *Queen of Clippers*, *Competitor* and so on. In this year, freight rates were beginning to edge downwards in the California trade so that it was the last year of the great clipper ship boom.

During 1853, Canadian shipyards launched many fine ships in the 1,200 to 1,500 tons range which were either built to the order of Liverpool owners or else on speculation and then sent to that port where they could be sure of getting sold. One of

[**Opposite top**] *Lines and general arrangement of the* Flying Fish, *which was built in 1851 at East Boston by Donald McKay, with dimensions of 207.0 ft × 39.6 ft × 22.0 ft and 1505 tons o.m. She has very fine waterlines but not too much rise of floor and the deck layout is standard. Reconstruction by H. S. Scott for Model Shipways of Bogota, N.J.* (Model Shipways).

[**Opposite bottom**] *Mast and rigging plan of the* Flying Fish *showing the yards at the positions to which they were lowered when the sails were furled, although no sails are included on this plan. No stunsail booms nor their fittings are included. Reconstructed by H. S. Scott for Model Shipways of Bogota, New Jersey.* (Model Shipways).

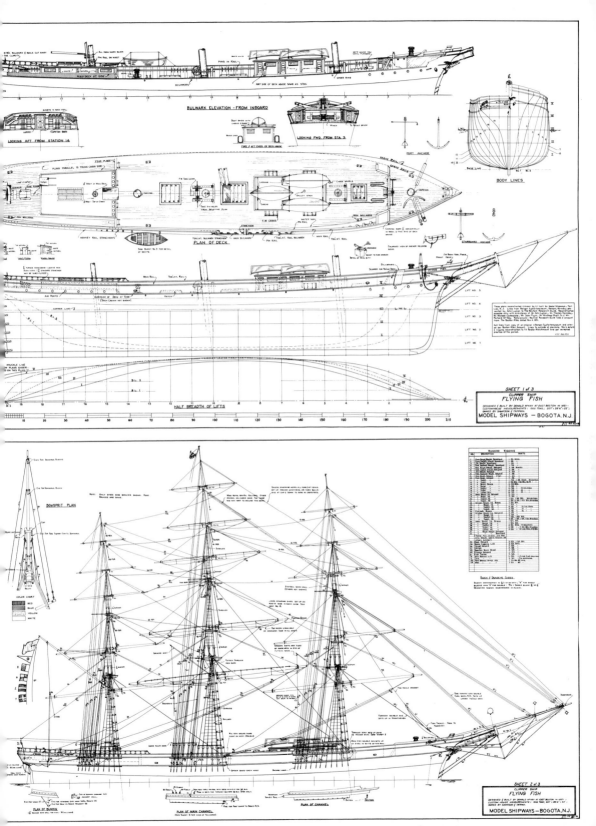

BULWARK ELEVATION - FROM INDOARD

LOOKING AFT FROM STATION 14

LOOKING FWD FROM STA. 3

BODY LINES

PLAN OF DECK

HALF BREADTH OF LIFTS

SHEET 1 of 3
CLIPPER SHIP
FLYING FISH

DESIGNED & BUILT BY DONALD M·KAY AT EAST BOSTON IN 1851
CUSTOMHOUSE MEASUREMENTS : 1505 TONS ; 207'-39'4'-22';
OWNED BY SAMPSON & TAPPAN.

MODEL SHIPWAYS - BOGOTA, N.J.

BOWSPRIT PLAN

COLOR CHART
RED
BLUE
YELLOW
WHITE

PLAN OF BUMKIN

PLAN OF MAIN CHANNEL

PLAN OF CHANNEL

SHEET 2 of 3
CLIPPER SHIP
FLYING FISH

DESIGNED & BUILT BY DONALD M·KAY AT EAST BOSTON IN 1851
CUSTOM HOUSE MEASUREMENTS : 1505 TONS, 207'-39'4'-22';
OWNED BY SAMPSON & TAPPAN.

MODEL SHIPWAYS - BOGOTA, N.J.

the finest was the *Star of the East* which William and Richard Wright launched from their St John yard. She measured 204 ft 9 in × 36 ft 6 in × 22 ft 0 in and 1,219 tons; her main yard was 89 ft long. Her maiden passage occupied 76 days to Melbourne and she came home via China. *Mermaid* was another fine St John ship which the Black Ball Line chartered; she sailed the day before the clipper *Red Jacket* but took five days longer on the passage, being 74 days to Melbourne. *Prince of the Seas* of 1,427 tons, built by Smith, builder of *Marco Polo*, claimed a day's run of 431 miles but it has not been verified. The *Guiding Star* was considered a lofty ship and was chartered by the Golden Line in 1853 for £12,000; she went missing the following year with 480 passengers when bound for Melbourne, and it was supposed she had either struck an iceberg when running her easting down, south of 50° latitude, or become embayed in an icefield. When clippers sailed far south on a great circle course, the ill-clad emigrants were often almost frozen to death in the intense cold and biting winds as the skippers drove their ships eastwards for Melbourne.

One of the few Canadian clippers for which plans exist is the *Oliver Lang*, said to have been designed by the naval architect of that name. She was built by Walter Brown at St John of 1,236 tons. She had moderate deadrise, slight tumblehome and very sharp ends; the long, hollow entrance was longer than the run. Her profile was old-fashioned with a heavy square stern. In 1855 she took 87 days out to Melbourne from Liverpool on her maiden passage, the delay apparently being occasioned by her having gone

The clipper ship N. B. Palmer *at anchor in a Chinese port. As this is a broadside photograph and the yards are 'squared', they are only seen end-on in foreshortened appearance. This view clearly indicates the distance by which the yards are set in front of the masts, and the manner in which the masts are 'doubled'. The relative thickness of differing parts of the rigging is worth noting.* (A. J. Nesdall).

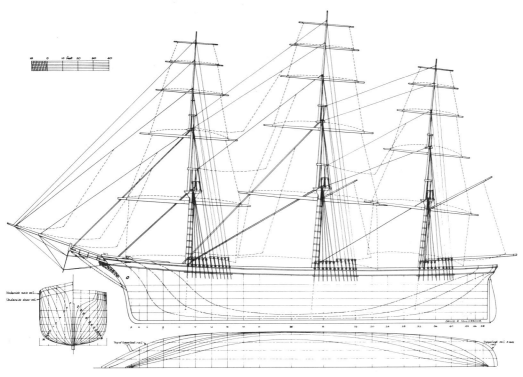

The proportion of masts and sails to the hull is clearly demonstrated in this plan of the extreme clipper Red Jacket. *Built in 1853 with a tonnage of 2305 tons and a length of 251.2 ft, she was designed by Samuel Pook. Plan drawn by David R. MacGregor.* (Author).

ashore in Bantry Bay, Ireland, en route to Liverpool; but she was finally got off and repaired. She was obviously a ship that liked the land as in 1859 she was either run ashore near Wellington or was blown ashore in a squall.

The year of 1853 had been crowded with momentous events in the annals of American clipper ships, with new records being made and splendid new ships being launched. Carl Cutler records that some 270 clippers had been built in the decade beginning in 1843, and that half of these were built in the year 1853. With so many ships available, the freight market was starting to wilt and the clippers were being sold abroad, especially to Great Britain and Germany, or else they were being forced to load guano or carry coolies or even slaves. Twenty American clippers loaded tea in China for British ports. The building of new clippers for the California trade continued as orders had been placed in 1853, but by 1854 orders for new ships were down to a trickle.

Donald McKay must therefore have been pleased to have secured an order from James Baines of Liverpool to build four ships for the Australian run. The first ship was the *Lightning*, delivered in March 1854. She was the last really large extreme clipper to be built in America. She had a very long hollow entrance with maximum beam abreast of the mainmast; the run was sharp and hollow, but shorter; there was not much deadrise but the bilges were very rounded and there was noticeable tumblehome. The bow was typically austere and adorned by a figurehead 'plastered on', as Basil Lubbock once put it. Measurements gave 237.5 ft (on deck) × 44.0 ft × 23.0 ft and 2,084 tons. The sail plan was very square and the main yard measured 95 ft; skysails on fore and mizen masts, with which she was not designed, were later added in England. Another English addition was the filling in of the concavity in the long entrance which was done by the 'Wood Butchers of Liverpool' prior to her third voyage, but part of it was washed away and the remainder removed in Melbourne.

Under the command of James N. Forbes, she crossed to Liverpool in only 13 days 20 hours land to land, her biggest day's run being 436 miles on 1 March 1854. Her maiden passage to Melbourne extended to 77 days owing to light winds. Leaving Melbourne again on 20 August, Forbes drove the clipper before the strong westerly winds towards Cape Horn often logging 18 and 19 knots and carrying-on in the most reckless manner so that it was hardly surprising that he lost the fore topsail yard and every other yard above on the foremast when eight days out. But new spars were quickly made from the spares she carried, and Cape Horn was passed 19 days 1 hour from Port Philip Heads. The passage occupied only 63 days 16 hours from the Heads to Point Lynas and 64 days 3 hours to Liverpool.

The racing between *Red Jacket* and *Lightning* was described in the *Australia and New Zealand Gazette* as a 'Great Ocean Regatta'; it gave the former's time out and back including detention in port as 164 days, but only 162 for the latter, which thus won the 'first heat' with two days to spare.

The *Lightning* made many more fast passages, such as 69 days and 6 hours to Port Philip Heads in 1857. Captain Enright, who had her for four years, received a salary of £1,000 per annum—unheard-of pay for a master in those days. She caught fire on 30 October 1869 at Geelong and was scuttled.

The next of McKay's quartette was the *Champion of the Seas* which was launched in April 1854; *James Baines* was the third to be completed, and she was launched in July. The former had long sharp ends, but more evenly balanced than *Lightning* and with even less deadrise; *James Baines* was a cross between these two, but her stem had more rake. The *Donald McKay*, launched in January 1855, was an enormous medium clipper and she was powerful enough to withstand hard driving and make good passages in strong winds being an ideal ship for the Australia trade.

James Baines was longer and deeper than *Lightning* with dimensions of 251 ft 5 in (on deck) × 46 ft 2 in × 29 ft 0 in and 2,275 tons (British measurement). She had a larger sail area than *Lightning* with a main yard of 100 ft; she also sported a main moonsail. *Champion of the Seas* was about the same size as *James Baines* but had a 95 ft main yard. Everything about these clippers was on a vast scale and their high freeboard kept the decks comparatively dry.

Maiden voyages are sometimes the peak of a ship's career, and this was certainly true of *James Baines*. On her run across the Atlantic she established the record from Boston to Liverpool in 12 days 6 hours to Rock Light, sometimes logging 20 knots. Under Captain Charles McDonnell, she sailed from Liverpool on 10 December 1854 and reached Melbourne on 12 February, 64 days later, or 63 days 18 hours from Rock Light to Hobson's Bay. A time of 58 days land to land was claimed. Her biggest day's run was 423 miles. Her return passage was of 69½ days, which was a remarkable performance. In 1856 she attained a speed of 21 knots. She was destroyed by fire in 1858 at Liverpool.

The Aberdeen-built clipper *Thermopylae*, on her maiden passage from London to Melbourne in 1868–69, passed Start Point on 8 November and sighted Cape Otway at the entrance to Hobson's Bay on 7 January 1869, the elapsed time being 60 days 3 hours. The Melbourne *Argus* published the abstract log and it was never queried at the

This remarkable photograph of the Archer *shows her in dry-dock at Foochow, probably after she went ashore in the River Min in 1865. Built in 1853 of 1095 tons n.m., she regularly traded to California and the Far East. At the outer ends of the fore and main lower yards can be discerned the circular irons through which the stunsail booms passed; and hinged back beside the hull from the fore channels is a lower stunsail boom. The lighter part of the hull, looking like a stone wall, is her copper sheathing. (A. J. Nesdall).*

time, so it seems incomprehensible that Carl Cutler should comment in his most useful reference work, *Five Hundred Sailing Records of American Built Ships*, published in 1952: 'I have found no evidence that the 60 day runs of the *Thermopylae*, reported by Lubbock, were ever made'. But the fact is that *Thermopylae*'s passage *is* the record run from London to Melbourne.

A point of interest is that all the sustained bursts of speed and fast passages by these three clippers which McKay built were made when the ships were commanded by British masters and under British ownership. The British for their part have in the past

The famous clipper **Young America** *berthed at the North Point Dock, San Francisco, in 1872. She was a very lofty ship, crossing skysail yards on each mast. Many captains thought it enhanced the ship's appearance not to lower the upper topsail yards close down on to the lower ones, when in port.* (San Francisco Maritime Museum).

contended that the great speeds were just tall stories by Yankees intent on blowing their own trumpets, little realizing that their own countrymen had a hand in it. American captains were well aware of the advantage of good press coverage and frequently provided reporters with detailed accounts of the ship's construction and prowess, which editors were only too pleased to print.

The *Champion of the Seas* may not have made any passages as fast as the other two ships, but her biggest day's run has never been beaten. This was of 465 miles made on 12 December 1854 under Captain Newlands which is an average of 20 knots throughout the day. This took place on her maiden passage to Melbourne which occupied 75 days.

Of other American ships built in 1854, Samuel Pook designed the *Ocean Telegraph* which Curtis built at Medford of 1,495 tons (1,214 new measurement); R. E. Jackson built the *Blue Jacket* at East Boston, and she made a passage of 69 days to Melbourne from Liverpool in 1855; and George Steers, who designed the schooner yacht *America*, designed and built the extreme clipper *Sunny South* at his yard at Williamsburg, New

York. Of 702 tons, she had an extremely long hollow entrance, similar in design to that of the iron clipper *Storm Cloud* which was launched the same year on the Clyde.

Ships too numerous to mention were being built in 1854 in Canada, but Wright's *White Star*, launched under the name of *Blue Jacket*, was a splendid example, measuring 284 ft long on deck and of 2,339 tons. The *Shalimar* of 1,402 tons and others like her were queens of the seas wherever they sailed or into whatever harbour they entered, and their arrival or departure was news.

The Australian gold rush helped to perpetuate the big American clippers for another year or two, and many ships sailed direct from American ports, employing Lieutenant Maury's charts and sailing directions to take advantage of the prevailing winds around the world, according to the season of the year. The Crimean War siphoned off a considerable amount of surplus tonnage and so artificially maintained freight rates, but when peace was declared in 1856 there was a glut of ships on the market, and new clippers were no longer wanted. Yet some of this breed were always being built, such as the *Andrew Jackson* of 1,679 tons which came out in 1855 and probably made the fastest passage ever performed under sail between New York and San Francisco, namely 89 days 4 hours in 1859. But the clippers built in their heyday still raced from port to port, and their deeds were still news.

The Beeston Castle *taking in her topgallants when inward bound to Liverpool with the pilot cutter on the right. She was built at Miramichi in 1857 of 1005 tons. The painting is signed 'J. & F. Tudgay'.* (Parker Gallery).

[**Above**] *The clipper* Golden State *pictured at Quebec in 1884 when rigged as a barque under the name of* Annie C. Maguire. *She was built in 1853 at New York of 1363 tons, and two years later made a passage of 90 days from Shanghai to New York. There were still irons on the fore topgallant yard to permit her to set royal stunsails.* (Peabody Museum of Salem).

[**Opposite**] *This daguerrotype shows the* Seaman's Bride *on the slip ready for launching at Baltimore in 1851. Her tonnage was 668. The upper trailboard is very deep, being a continuation of the bulwarks.* (Maryland Historical Society).

[**Below**] *A panorama of San Francisco Bay, in 1863 ; a full-rigged ship lies at anchor. She has single topsails and crosses skysail yards on each mast. The stunsail booms are triced up on the fore and main topsail yards.* (Courtesy of Robert A. Weinstein).

[**Above**] *A stylized lithograph by Currier & Ives of the* Sovereign of the Seas. *This extreme clipper was built in 1852 by Donald McKay.* (Parker Gallery).

[**Right**] *This photograph of the* Great Republic *must have been taken before 1862 because it was in this year that the jigger mast was removed. This is copied from a stereo view.* (Peabody Museum of Salem).

[**Above**] *A broadside view of the* Great Republic *taken at San Francisco in 1860. The stunsail booms on the lower yards are slung beneath the yards. The jibboom is hauled inboard on to the foc'sle head. The mainyard is 100 ft long.* (Peabody Museum of Salem).

[**Below**] *A rare photograph of the* Great Republic *as a three-masted full-rigged ship, with her fourth or 'jigger' mast removed.* (Peabody Museum of Salem).

The Dashing Wave, *built in 1853 at Portsmouth, New Hampshire of 104 tons new measurement (American), survived until 1920. In this picture taken about 1890, she is carrying timber, including a deck cargo of it, between Puget Sound and San Francisco into which trade she had fallen in the last two decades of the nineteenth century. Running before the wind, the ship is under easy sail and the foresail is about to be clewed up. With the anchor hanging from the cathead, she is probably going to take in sail before achoring. Her main skysail yard is out of the picture. (San Francisco Maritime Museum).*

Against a forest of masts and dwarfing men and horses on the quays, the clipper bow of the
Dreadnought, *carrying the figurehead of a winged dragon with its tail curling down the
stem, embodies all the romance that clings to this era. Nicknamed 'The Wild Boat of the
Atlantic', she averaged only 19 days on 20 passages made eastwards from New York.
Built in 1853 at Newburyport of 1413 tons, she was wrecked in 1869. In this picture, the
bowsprit has been run inboard, after slackening off some of the stays, which was a practice
commonly adopted when in port. Photograph taken 1862 at Wall Street Dock, New York
by Matthew Brady. (San Francisco Maritime Museum).*

[Above] *A photograph taken at Williamstown in 1866 with the clipper* Lightning *at anchor in the distance. The ships in the foreground have not been identified but they yield a good impression of the great length of the lower yards in relation to the breadth of the hull.* (The late D. M. Little).

[Opposite] *The clipper ship* Champion of the Seas *is almost certainly the ship photographed here in this daguerrotype by Southworth and Hawes of Boston. The scene is in Donald McKay's shipyard at Boston in 1854; the lower, topsail and topgallant yards are crossed and some of the sails bent; running rigging is rove; the Black Ball line flag flies at the main truck.* (Richard Parker).

[Below] *The* Lightning *on fire at Geelong in 1869; the foremast has fallen over the near side on fire. She was scuttled in 24 ft of water and later destroyed.* (The late A. D. Edwardes).

[**Above**] *Lying to a buoy in the River Thames is the* Royal Dane *which was built under the name of* Sierra Nevada *at Portsmouth, New Hampshire, in 1854 of 1616 tons, and with a with a length of 230 ft overall. It was in 1863 that her name was changed when the Black Ball Line bought her for £10,750. In this photograph by Gould of Gravesend, a canvas ventilator has been rigged just forward of the foremast.* (Author).

[**Below**] *This photograph of the* Empress *under full sail appears to be of the ship built by Paul Curtis at Boston in 1855 of 1293 tons. She was sold to Houlder Bros of Liverpool in 1863 and in 1877 became the German-owned* Elizabeth *of Bremen. It seems unlikely that any camera could capture such a picture prior to 1877, so it seems probable that she is here actually sailing under her German name.* (National Maritime Museum).

[**Above**] *Another clipper sold to British owners was the* Fatherland *which in 1860 was renamed* Swiftsure *when bought by R. & H. Green. Of 1326 tons she was built at Boston in 1854 by W. Hall. She must have been involved in some forgotten incident as her yards are askew, only three of her square sails are bent, water is being pumped over her side amidships, and there are two twin-funnelled tugs standing by on her starboard quarter. Two of her crew are climbing the main topmast rigging and others are on the foreyard, where the topmast stunsail boom has been triced up to allow them to work on the foresail.* (National Maritime Museum).

[Left] *The* Black Hawk *was one of William H. Webb's last clipper designs, being built in 1856 of 1109 tons. Her hollow entrance can be seen in this photograph. She was sold to Bremen owners in 1880.* (National Maritime Museum).

CHAPTER SIX

Clipper Brigs and Schooners after 1850

It has been argued that all the successful developments that became established in large ships were first tried out and proved in small vessels. This could certainly be true in the case of the Aberdeen clipper schooner *Scottish Maid* which was the forerunner of many British full-rigged ships of extreme form that appeared in the 1850s. Also, two earlier examples of fast-sailing types were the American pilot boat and the English cutter, and though both produced sizeable hulls on occasion, especially the cutter, each contributed to the development of clipper ships. The desire for speed which became evident in the clippers designed to race home with tea from China or rush prospectors out to the gold fields permeated all types of craft, so that it finally becomes hard to find examples of bluff-bodied schooners built after 1850. There was really no need to hurry cargoes of goods around the coasts faster than had been done previously, but competition and the ability to deliver more cargoes per annum were incentives towards higher profits. Even the brigs were less full-bodied and the increasing number of wet-docks where vessels could lie afloat, even at low water, meant that the flat-floored hull was no longer so vitally essential.

A smart, clean, good-looking schooner or brigantine with an enviable reputation for speed, a high class at Lloyd's Register and a record of delivering her cargo in good condition would be sure of getting a slightly higher rate of freight. The profit motive was behind every new departure in shipbuilding, and even if a clipper brig could carry less cargo than a full-bodied version, there was the probability that she could deliver one or more extra cargoes per annum due to her speed and abilities to go to windward. Stories are told of clippers in the fruit trade passing the anchored shipping in the Downs and then beating down the English Channel against strong westerly winds, loading their oranges in the Azores and running homewards up the Channel again some three weeks later to find the very same windbound host of ships straining at their anchors and not having earned their owners a penny.

The carriage of perishable cargoes, especially fresh fruit, fish, butter and cheese, the trade in opium between India and China, the avoidance of pirates and hazardous waters in Eastern Seas, as well as the carriage of passengers or livestock all demanded speed. Although sloops and cutters had been used in the fruit trade, they were increasingly relegated to more humble employment.

Shipbuilders at such ports as Salcombe, Dartmouth, Rye, Brixham and Ipswich specialized in clipper schooners for the citrus fruit trade which was at its peak in the 1840s and 1850s, but after 1870 the schooners were largely superseded by steamers. Oranges and lemons were discharged at London, Liverpool, Bristol and Southampton.

The brigantine Devonia *was built at Ipswich in 1865 for trade to South America. Of 161 tons, she would originally have had a shorter bowsprit with a separately fidded jibboom, and would also have crossed a royal yard, like* Juan de la Vega. *It is even possible that she began life with a single topsail instead of double ones.* (W. J. Cock).

The principal loading port was St Michaels in the Azores.

The fruit schooners, in addition to their large gaff sails, usually set a square topsail, topgallant and royal on the foremast, as well as a big square sail from the fore yard, and outside these four sails were stunsails, so that a two-masted schooner was virtually converted into a brigantine. After 1850, the masts were not raked so excessively but were still placed closer together than was the case after 1870. Some illustrations show them to carry a boat in davits between the masts as well as a long boat stowed on top of the main hatch. Right forward was the windlass and scuttle to the crew's foc'sle; close abaft the foremast was the galley; around the mainmast were the pumps, fife rail and cargo winch, and abaft it were the skylight to the saloon, the companion hatch to the after accommodation on which was the binnacle, and finally the wheel. The deck was flush from end to end, but there was occasionally a low deck forward between the stem and the pawl post. The ship's bell was on the top of the latter, and this post was so named because the three or four pawls which prevented the windlass barrel revolving backwards were fitted on it. This was the standard layout on schooners and brigs, but the latter might occasionally have a raised quarter-deck.

Decks were holystoned to a light cream colour although coasting vessels might paint their's; deck fittings might be varnished or painted. Paint was usually red, blue or green and extended to the inside of bulwarks and base of masts; galleys were often painted white. Externally, hulls were usually black or occasionally green, with a white or gold stripe flowing from the upper edge of the trail board. A so-called 'clipper' bow was normal, graced by a figurehead, either bust or full length, with a carved trail board several feet in length. There was also some carving at the stern: a carved rope, arching over the name and port of registry, was popular, and it terminated in a small carved design on each quarter.

In hull-form the clipper schooners of Devon and Cornwall often possessed a sharp convex entrance, with a longer run that was noticeably concave; there was appreciable deadrise with rounded bilges, but the floors were never steep after 1850; there was usually a long over-hanging counter, and a square stern was retained for many years. Other parts of the country had hulls with more balanced ends, sometimes with greater deadrise, but schooners were always faced with the possibility of having to stand moderately upright beside a quay wall when the tide ebbed away. The fruit schooners and others that went deep-water were all copper sheathed—indeed coppering was a sure sign of a 'blue water' trader.

Pictures of Salcombe schooners such as *Queen of the South* (1850 of 120 tons), and *Zouave* (1855 of 127 tons) illustrate the type of craft described. The *Zouave*'s figurehead was carved by an Italian living in Plymouth and represented one of the French troops who were cutting such a dash in the Crimean war, as Michael Bouquet tells us in *No Gallant Ship*. Another Salcombe vessel was the *Bezaleel*, launched the year after *Zouave*, and she is recorded by Basil Lubbock in *Last of the Windjammers* (Vol I) as taking only $5\frac{1}{2}$ days between St Michaels and Liverpool. He records another schooner, the *Elinor* of 129 tons, sailing from London Bridge, in 1869, to St Michaels and back in 17 days.

One of the last surviving fruiters was the *Brooklands*, built as the *Susan Vittery* in 1859 at Dartmouth. She foundered in 1953 off the Irish Coast.

Amongst so many two-masted vessels of varying rigs, all of which had moderately fine lines so that they could weather the coasts and narrow seas which they navigated more frequently than the deepwater ships, it becomes difficult to single out any vessels which were of extreme clipper hull-form unless whole ranges of plans and models are available for inspection. And this is definitely not the case. The smaller vessels had even less recorded about them than their larger sisters, and as the yards which built them have mostly disappeared without trace, the survival of plans or models is accidental.

I have taken lines off half-models and traced builders' plans, but it is rare for a lines plan and sail plan to have survived for the same vessel. In the case of the schooner *Express* which was built at Glasson Dock in 1860, there was an exception, as the half-model and builders' cost account had survived, and a sail plan showing her converted from a two to a three-master was discovered. Thus the ingredients for reconstruction were all present. She did not have a lofty rig, but the main boom was a long spar, and the square topsail and topgallant on the foremast gave a good area of square canvas. When given a mizen mast, the mainmast was not moved, but the main boom was cut in half, thus making the main and mizen gaff sails tall narrow sails.

Another case where a reconstruction was possible concerns the schooner *Rhoda Mary* whose lines I took off with Basil Greenhill's assistance in 1949. She was then lying in the mud at Hoo on the River Medway. She was built in 1868 at Yard Point, Restronguet Creek, near Truro, by John Stephens, from a half-model carved by William Ferris. It was remarkable to have been able to record such a fine-lined schooner, but her spar dimensions are entirely reconstructed, with the exception of the mizen lower mast, main topmast, and spike bowsprit. Her dimensions were

The schooner Queen of the South *looks every inch a clipper in this painting by an Italian artist. She forms a good example of the sleek craft owned in South Devon in the fifties and sixties. She was built at Salcombe in 1850 of 120 tons, with a length of* $82\frac{1}{2}$ *ft. (J. Fairweather).*

101.2 ft × 21.9 ft × 11.0 ft and 118 tons. She began life with two masts but a mizen was added in 1898. She was never in the fruit trade nor did she go deep-water, but kept to the British home trade in which she was reckoned to have been one of the five fastest schooners, according to seamen questioned by Basil Greenhill in the 1930s and 1940s.

The other fast schooners were reckoned to be the *Katie Cluett*, built in Stephens' yard at Fowey in 1876 of 126 tons, and designed by Peter Ferris, younger brother of William who designed *Rhoda Mary*; next came the three-masted schooner *Trevellas*, built on the shore under the high cliffs near St Agnes, Cornwall, in 1876; the *Perseverance*, built at Fowey in 1862 as a schooner but converted to a brigantine in 1881; last came the *Result*, but she falls outside the clipper era as she was launched in 1893.

Fowey has always had a reputation for building fast-sailing craft and some fine examples were launched in the 1870s, such as the barquentine *Ocean Swell* (1875 of 187 tons by Stephens) which voyaged to South America and South Africa; the schooner *Thetis* (1873 of 173 tons) and the brigantine *Undine* (1875 of 174 tons), both built by Butson and of very similar dimensions. The latter was said to be a fine-lined craft which could only sail with ballast in her hold and is reputed to have gone from Bristol to St

Michaels and back in 19 days. Even in that decade, vessels such as these were accustomed to set stunsails on their regular passages to increase their sail area.

Another builder in the south of England who specialized in clipper schooners was the firm of J. & R. White of Cowes who produced the opium clippers *Nina* (1851 of 115 tons), *Eamont* (1852 of 158 tons), and *Wild Dayrell* (1854 of 158 tons). The latter's portrait was engraved in the *Illustrated London News* in 1855 and the caption commented on her 'yacht-like appearance', and then continued:

'She has a heavy and most complete armament for protection against the swarms of pirates that now infest the Coast of China, and, in the event of coming athwart [the] hawse of those junks, her "Long Tom amidships" will, no doubt, tell a tale.'

Like the other two schooners, she was owned by Dent & Co.

Another builder to design and construct clipper schooners for the opium trade was Alexander Hall, situated at the opposite end of the country in Aberdeen. In the 1840s he had already built the *Torrington* for the trade and in the next decade came the *Vindex*, a smart vessel of 229 tons built in 1855. Dimensions of the latter were 109.7 ft × 23.6 ft × 13.2 ft; her main boom measured 60 ft and she carried a royal yard on the fore mast. She cost £18.50 per ton based on 264 tons o.m. Unfortunately no lines plan of her has survived. The following year Hall built the 115-ton schooner *Salamander* as a yacht for the Earl of Selkirk at a cost of £5,000; three years later she made the passage out to Hong Kong in 110 days and was sold to become an opium clipper. However, the end of the opium clippers was already in sight as steamers were gradually replacing them.

In 1855, Alexander Hall & Sons launched the barquentine *Kelpie* of 118 tons for Charles Horsfall & Sons of Liverpool to run in their trade to Gambia, so she probably had to be fast and heavily-canvassed to survive that treacherous coast. She was a queer sort of barquentine because her fore lower mast was as long as a schooner's, but the fore topgallant mast was fidded; this resulted in a very deep fore course. There was a single yard listed for the mainmast and it was conceivably slung from the lower mast hounds like a lower yard.

Not so many two-masters were built by Hall in the fifties and sixties, but in 1871 he launched the attractive brigantine *Juan de la Vega*. James Henderson has drawn out her lines from the builder's offset table, while the original sail and spar plan has been used to reconstruct a more complete plan. She was built for Spanish owners in Corunna with measurements of 100.3 ft × 23.95 ft × 12.2 ft and 172 tons; she cost £2,780. The hull lines show great fineness in the ends and there is marked deadrise. The masts have considerable rake for this date; although four-sided staysails were common, the arrangement between the masts seems unusual; no doubt, stunsails would have been set on the foremast.

There is a model in the Science Museum, London, of Hall's barquentine *John Wesley* which was built in 1867 of composite construction for the Wesleyan Missionary Society. This gives a good idea of hull-form that looks similar to *Juan de la Vega*, but with less deadrise. There is a raised quarter-deck and an elaborate companionway leading down to the after accommodation. Although the masts and yards were made by the Museum staff to the lengths specified by the builder, the rigging was done in about 1910 and some of it is unreliable, particularly the stays from the main and mizen masts. Another of Hall's missionary vessels was the *John Williams* built in 1868; she was a small barque of only 200 tons, or 38 tons smaller than the *John Wesley*, and her lines and sail plan are reproduced as Figure 266 in *Fast Sailing Ships*.

Lying at anchor in Salcombe harbour is the schooner Zouave, *built at the port in 1855. The yards on her fore topmast can just be made out, including the stunsail booms triced up above her topsail yard. There is a standing gaff on the fore, and the sail is brailed into the mast; on the main, the gaff lowers on top of the long boom. She is described in the text. (J. Fairweather).*

There were numerous other shipyards in north-east Scotland, producing barquentines, schooners and small barques, such as Stephen of Peterhead who built the barquentine *Lord of the Isles* of 317 tons in 1869 for the China trade; and James Geddie of Garmouth who built the barquentine *Union* in 1867 of 234 tons for Murray of Portsoy, who placed her in the Mediterranean trade. How enterprising of shipowners in small Scottish ports to send their ships out for cargoes to far distant waters, and it speaks highly of the trust placed in the masters of such craft who held all the business in their hands, and had the responsibility of finding lucrative cargoes. Of course, the masters usually held some of the sixty-four shares into which the ownership of every vessel, whether small or great, was divided—just as it is today.

Many barquentines were at this date still described in the pages of Lloyd's Register as 'schooner', and some authorities even called them 'three-masted brigantines'. For

the purposes of masters' certificates granted by the Board of Trade, they were classed as 'square rigged', whereas brigantines were denoted as 'fore-and-aft'.

The Aberdeen bow was copied in north European countries in brigs and schooners. A lines plan exists in Frode Holm-Petersen's collection of the clipper brig *Harmonie* which Julius Jensen built at Troense, Denmark, in the 1850s with considerable forward rake to the stem; the hull had a sharp convex entrance and a long convex run, without much hollow; there was also marked deadrise. The two masts raked aft to a considerable extent. No sail plan exists. Illustrations suggest that some barques also had this form of bow. There was also interest in Holland where a copy has been found of an unidentified Aberdeen schooner dated 1846.

In Canada, at La Have, Nova Scotia, Ebenezer Moseley committed a design on to paper in the 1850s for a flush-decked clipper brig; dimensions given on the plan are 100 ft keel, 26 ft moulded breadth, and 13 ft 9 in depth of hold. The waterlines were moderately sharp but without much deadrise; on the other hand, the forward rake of the stem was very pronounced above the waterline, and the total length of the rake measured 17 ft 6 in.

Of the models in the National Watercraft Collection at the Smithsonian Institution

[**Left**] *Unloading cargo aboard the* Susan Vittery. *She was a two-masted schooner built at Dartmouth in 1859, but later converted to three masts. Her name became changed to* Brooklands *and she survived until lost in 1953. Here, the cargo winch is close against the fore side of the main-mast with a fresh water tank abaft it.* (R. H. C. Gillis).

[**Right**] *Abandoned in the mud at Hoo on the River Medway, the shapely bows of the schooner* Rhoda Mary *recall her days at sea. She was built in 1868 near Devoran, Cornwall, as a two-masted schooner. Her stem originally carried a figurehead but the trail boards are still in position.* (Author).

which Howard Chapelle described in his book published in 1960, none of the brigantines and schooners which he measured and drew in plan form seem to be of really clipper hull-form, although they would rate as medium clippers. In all of them, carrying capacity seems important, and fine lines are sacrificed to this. Chapelle describes the brigantine *J. W. Parker*, which was built at Belfast, Maine, in 1874, as the 'final development of the American trading brigantine, combining swift sailing, weatherliness, and good handling qualities with excellent cargo capacity'.

When the American three-masted fore-and-aft schooner *Eckford Webb* visited Glasgow in 1856, Alexander Stephen & Sons took her on their slipway and preserved a copy of her sail plan in their files. Pure fore-and-aft schooners like her were called 'terns' in Canada and America; their masts were of equal height and on the mizen was the largest gaff sail. The first one came out in 1849 in America, but the first Canadian appeared ten years later with the name of *Zebra*, having been built at La Have. Those with shallow-draft hulls were usually fitted with a centreboard. One such tern was the *Phantom* of 210 tons, built at New York in 1853 by George Steers, and when she visited Appledore, North Devon, in 1857, her centreboard was removed.

Other examples of three-masted schooners in Great Britain during the 1850s include the arrival at Newcastle in 1851 of the Portuguese schooner *Emma* of 192 tons, described as 'quite a yacht'; the construction at Dundee in 1854 by Gourlay Bros of the narrow iron-hulled *Alma* of 190 tons with dimensions of 121.6 ft × 20.0 ft × 9.4 ft, intended for a rapid voyage to Melbourne, and probably therefore of ultra-sharp hull-form; and the conversion and lengthening at Guernsey in 1852 of the *Aurora* from a two into a three three mast schooner.

At Shoreham in Sussex, James B. Balley launched the *Wild Dayrell*—not to be confused with the opium clipper built at Cowes the previous year—in August 1856. Comments, probably from the local newspapers, were quoted by Henry Cheal in his book on Shoreham shipping, which described her as 'of a Yankee three mast schooner rig' and 'built on hollow waterlines, a principle previously avoided at Shoreham'. She was named after the horse that won the Derby in 1855, and was intended to sail fast in the coasting trade. However, on her maiden voyage 'she rolled away all her gaffs and booms' and put into Plymouth to refit. Her dimensions were 136.0 ft × 24.2 ft × 14.5 ft and 310 tons, and she had two rider keelsons in addition to a side keelson and bilge keelson, all indicative of the builder's attempt to keep her sharp form from hogging. She was sheathed with zinc.

Another three-masted schooner came from Balley's yard in 1856: this was the *Osprey* of 220 tons, costing £3,164, which works out as £14.38 per ton. Three-masted schooners increased in popularity in the 1860s although the adequate staying of the mizen mast was not satisfactorily resolved until the lower mast was equal in height to the main lower mast. This enabled a stay to go to the main lower mast head and avoid the peak of the main gaff; in doing so, it obviated the need for the stays from the mizen down each side of the mainsail to the bulwarks by the main shrouds, which required constant slacking off or tightening up, depending on which tack the schooner was lying.

[**Above**] *Built by Alexander Hall & Sons at Aberdeen in 1856, the* Salamander *lies in the harbour newly completed as a yacht for the Earl of Selkirk, at a cost of £5000. She became an opium clipper three years later and sailed out to Hong Kong in 110 days. She is reputed to have eventually become a Portuguese slaver.* (J. Henderson).

[**Opposite**] *The artist has almost treated this picture as a sail plan; indeed, he may have been furnished with one by the master, Captain W. King. All the sail cloths and rigging are clearly shown. The four-sided staysails are typical of the sixties. Named* Katie, *this brigantine was built at Rye in 1866 of 195 tons for Balkwill & Co of Salcombe. Seven or eight members of the crew are lining the rail, the master has got his telescope to his eye, and the ship's cat is sitting on the counter.*

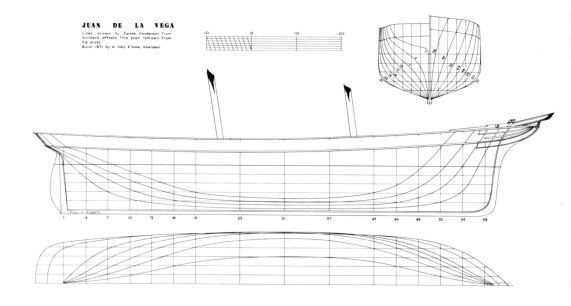

JUAN DE LA VEGA
Lines drawn by James Henderson from
builders offsets This plan redrawn from
his draft.
Built 1871 by A. Hall & Sons, Aberdeen.

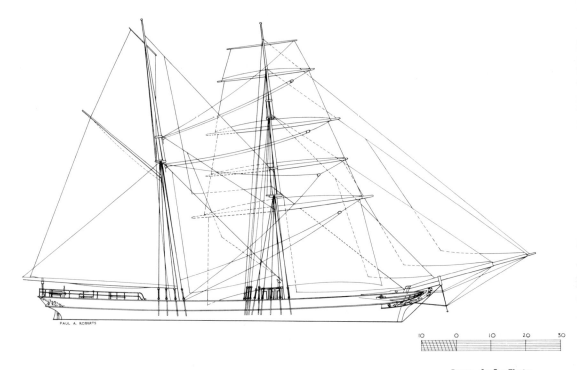

Juan de La Vega

Reconstructed from Builder's Sail Plan

[**Opposite top**] *Lines plan of the brigantine* Juan de la Vega, *built by A. Hall & Sons at Aberdeen in 1871 for Spanish owners. This plan was drawn by Paul Roberts based on the draught prepared from the builder's offsets by James Henderson.* (Author).

[**Opposite bottom**] *Sail plan of the* Juan de la Vega *drawn by Paul Roberts from the builder's plan. This is the standard sail plan for a brigantine built after 1870, although the spacing between the masts was often greater, the rake to the masts not so pronounced, and the staysails from the mainmast not so voluminous.* (Author).

[**Below**] *The barquentine* Lord of the Isles *lies in Peterhead Harbour. A particular feature is the excessive rake forward of her stem with its elaborately carved trail board. She was in the China trade, having been built in 1869.* (Peterhead Library and Arbuthnot Museum).

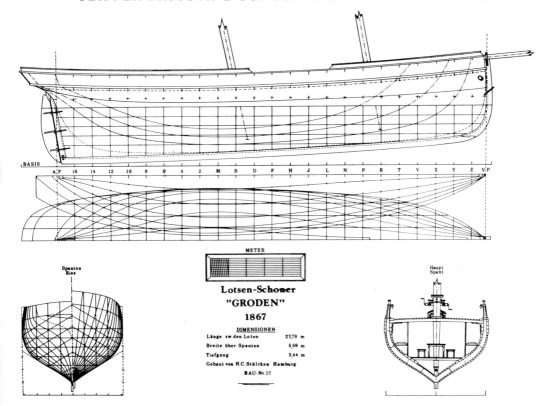

METER

Lotsen-Schooner
"GRODEN"
1867

DIMENSIONEN

Länge zw.den Loten	23,79 m
Breite über Spanten	5,59 m
Tiefgang	3,44 m
Gebaut von H.C.Stülcken Hamburg	
BAU-Nr.17	

[**Above**] *Lines plan of the pilot schooner* Groden, *built at Hamburg by H. C. Stülcken in 1867. She has great deadrise and fine waterlines, especially in the entrance. Plan drawn by Peter Rückert.* (Author).

[**Opposite top**] *This slightly indistinct picture of the barquentine* Caroline *is included to show the cloud of canvas set by such a vessel in the clipper ship era, including a fore skysail. Stunsail booms are drawn rigged-in, as she is close-hauled. She was built at Salcombe by Vivian in 1866 of 282 tons.* (J. Fairweather).

[**Opposite bottom**] *The schooner* Courant *was built at Kiel in 1856, and this picture was painted by H. Reimer of Kiel. She has a version of the 'Aberdeen clipper bow'.* (Author).

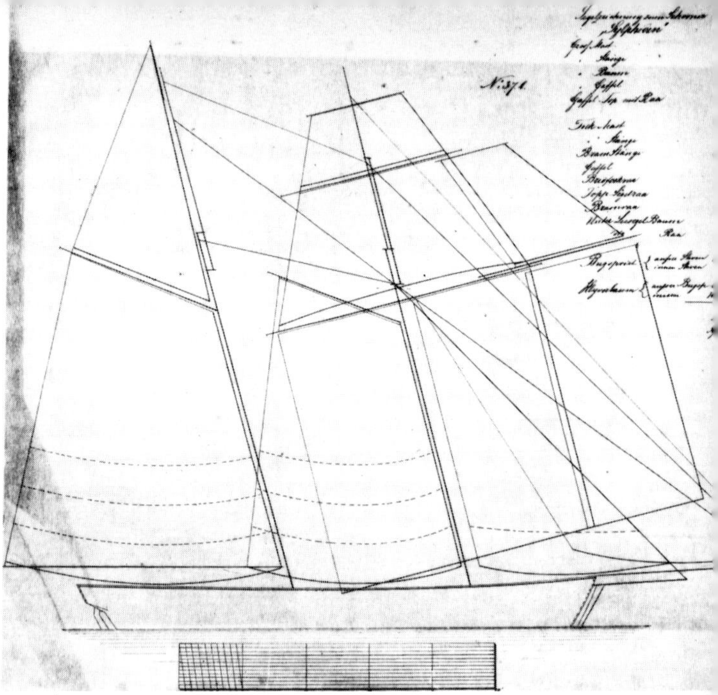

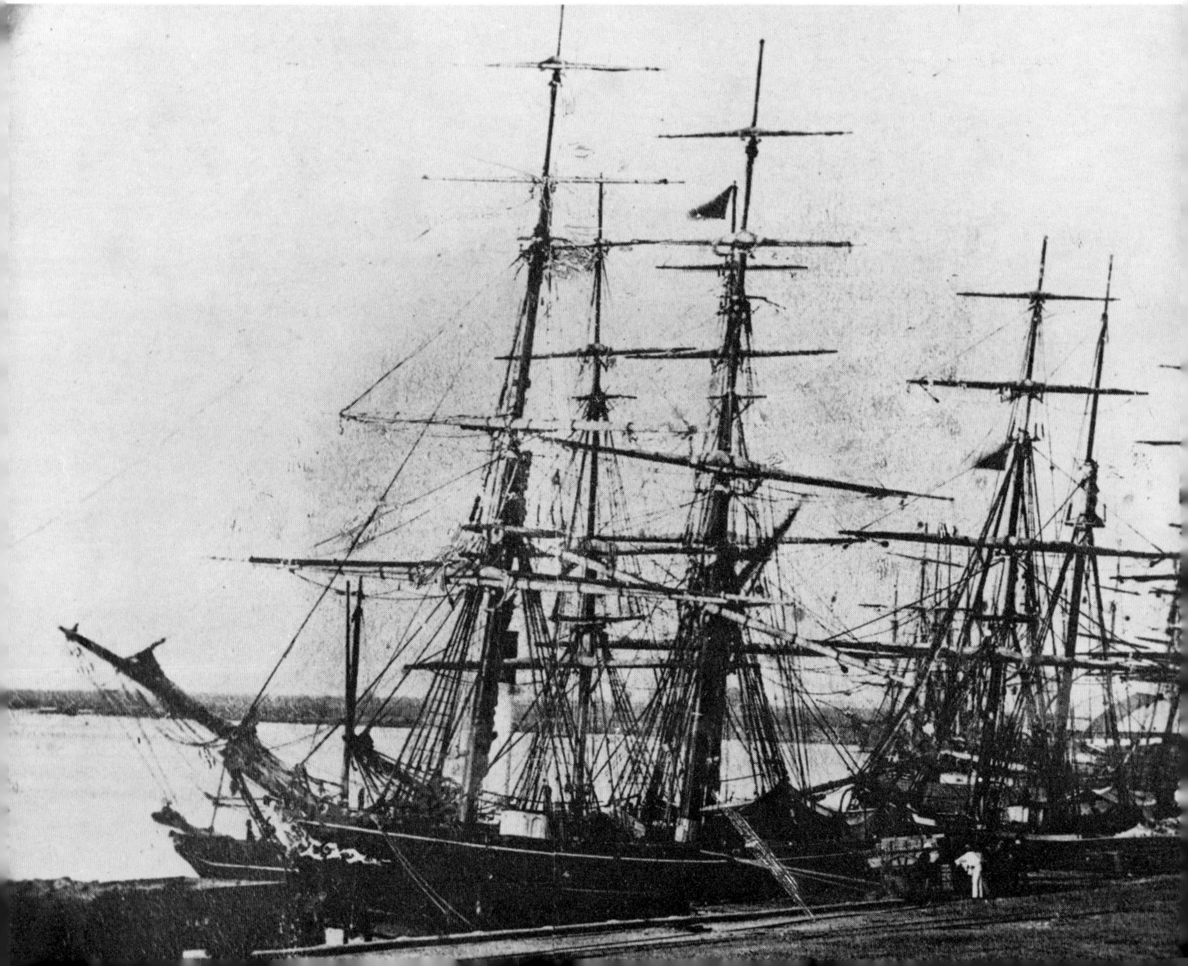

[**Above**] *This painting shows the American schooner* Wm. L. Cogswell *in the Mediterranean. The passaree booms to which the clews of the square sail, set from the fore yard, could be hauled out, are hinged upwards each side of the foremast.* (Parker Gallery).

[**Opposite top**] *A sail plan in outline of the schooner* Sylphiden *which was traced at Copenhagen in 1860 by G. Hillman. The most likely vessel of this name was built in 1854 at Nakskow, Denmark, but identification is not positive. Her fore topgallant mast is stepped on the lower mast cap, abaft the topmast. A lines plan gives her very big deadrise but moderately convex waterlines.* (Maritime Museum, Newport News).

[**Opposite bottom**] *Brigs and brigantines at Queen's Wharf, Port Adelaide, in December 1863. In the foreground is the brig* Elisa Corry, *built of iron at Stockton in 1856 and of 216 tons; outside her is the brig* Gazelle; *astern of these two is the brigantine* Active; *followed by the brig* Nile. *Copied from photograph in possession of Mrs Walker.* (Author).

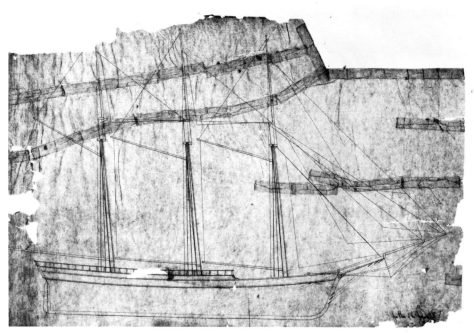

HUNTRESS

[**Above**] *A brig called* Teazer *under sail off Sandy Hook. Compare this with a barque of the same name reproduced on page 145. The brig has single topsails set, and they have Cunningham's roller-reefing gear fitted; the topgallants are very deep sails; the main boom is extremely long; there is a flying jibboom fitted.* (Peabody Museum of Salem).

[**Opposite top**] *Sail plan of the 'tern' or three-masted schooner* Eckford Webb *which was built by Eckford Webb at New York in 1855, with a length of 130 ft. She had a broad hull with sharp ends and claimed a speed of 16 knots.* (Author).

[**Opposite bottom**] *The schooner* Huntress *entering Malta harbour in 1864. She was built two years before at Salcombe by Vivian and owned by Balkwill, with a tonnage of 176. A longer jibboom would have been expected and altogether the hull looks short for the amount of canvas carried.* (J. Fairweather).

CHAPTER SEVEN

European Clippers after 1850

After the British Navigation Laws were repealed in 1849, ships of all nationalities were quick to take advantage of the increased trade in carrying goods to British ports. This freeing of trade restrictions was copied by Holland in 1850, and in 1857 Norway cancelled the duty previously paid on ships purchased abroad. In the 1860s France opened her colonial ports to international shipping and later her ports at home. But in the early 1850s it seemed that everything was falling into the American's lap as their large clippers which had discharged the prospectors in California found it was an ideal situation to have China tea waiting to be loaded on the other side of the Pacific. European ships, on the other hand, had no ready-made trade which took them to the Pacific, apart from the Dutch, whose own colonies provided the needed impetus. London retained its role as the entrepôt of the China tea trade, and imports from the Continent were generally made through London, rather than in ships sailing direct from China. But direct participation in the Australian gold rush was possible for Continental ships as many prospectors desired to sail from their own countries; in addition, British ships could not provide all the tonnage needed, and so many Dutch and several German ships were chartered by British companies.

Of all marine artists, Jacob Spin (1806–75) of Amsterdam has probably bestowed more impressions of speed and clipper looks on his ships than anyone else. There is usually a good rake to the masts; several stunsails are set, from whichever direction the wind is blowing; all the sails are full of wind; ensigns and signal flags are hoisted; the crew is busy on deck or aloft; and the ship is slashing through the water. Several of the clippers which he painted were rigged as brigs such as the *Candati* (1863) or *De Engel* (1864), both of which have double topsails. But one remembers him best by his full-rigged ships such as the *Voorlichter* which he portrayed with six square sails on each mast, royal stunsails on fore and main, and even stunsails on the mizen.

In his book *De Clippers*, Anno Teenstra lists names of clipper ships in the Appendix, and a few of them were built in other countries such as the *Electra* which had begun life as the American clipper *Witch of the Wave*, and the *Bellona* which was built by Rickmers at Bremerhaven in 1855.

One of the principal shipbuilders in Holland was Fop Smit of Kinderdijk whose first clipper was the *California* of 1853, and who later constructed the famous *Noach I*. A sail plan of the latter has the sails billowing out in the breeze with the weather clews of the mainsail and crossjack clewed up; and it will be noticed how tall are the masts compared with the length of the hull. As she was built in 1857, it seems remarkable that she should have double topsails: either they must be of Howes' pattern, imported from

96

A typical painting by the artist J. Spin of the Dutch clipper Ternate *under a press of sail. She was built in 1855. The large spanker has no boom, but is sheeted to an outrigger, of which there was one on each quarter.* (Scheepvaart Museum, Amsterdam).

America; or else the drawing must have been done later in her life. In 1863 she made the outward passage from Holland to Batavia in 80 days port to port, or 71 days land to land. On the return passage, sailing from Batavia on 10 September, she was only 71 days from there to Brouwershaven or $65\frac{1}{2}$ days from Anjer to the English coast line, which is the record for a Dutch ship.

Jan Smit of Slikkerveer built numerous clippers including *Noach II*, launched in 1867 of 952 tons, and *Noach III*, built in 1869 of 1,117 tons, both being owned by Fop Smit Jnr of Rotterdam. Another famous ship was the *Kosmopoliet I*, built in 1855 at Dordrecht by C. Gips & Son of 753 tons; a rigged model shows her with skysails on each mast and a very lofty rig, long jibboom and flying jibboom, but a shortish hull. There appears to be a fair amount of deadrise. The Dutch were apparently fond of continuing the name of a successful ship in later vessels; so we get a *Kosmopoliet II*, built in 1864 of 1,078 tons and yet a third of this name built in 1871. Each were built by Gips & Son. A picture of the second ship has the letters 'K II' painted on the fore lower topsail. The largest wooden sailing ship ever built in Holland was the *Liberaal* of 2,062 tons, built in 1872 by Jan Smit.

A large number of Dutch ships and barques were sailing to Sydney and Melbourne in 1852–53, and of the smaller craft, one was the three-masted schooner *Mary Goddard* which in 1853 took 92 days to Port Philip Heads from Liverpool.

Another schooner was the remarkable *Argo*, built in 1854 at Rotterdam by Rotterdam's Welvaren of 537 tons. Her rig was most unusual, because she had four masts. A painting done in 1858 by Spin shows that on the fore and main masts she carried lower, topsail, topgallant and royal yards, but no yards on the mizen and jigger masts. The fore and main lower masts were long and gaff sails are set, as well as square sails; the fore and main topmasts were poles without any topgallant masts fidded, thus making her a true schooner for the theorists; the mizen and jigger only set narrow gaff sails. She could be a 'jackass barque'; but the Bureau Veritas of 1870 called her a schooner with four masts.

There were not many clippers built in Norway, although plans of one, the *Hebe*, were published in the *Transactions of the Institution of Naval Architects* in London, 1866. This ship was built at Bergen in 1856 of 604 tons o.m. with dimensions of 143 ft 7 in (length on waterline) × 31 ft 8 in (maximum) × 19 ft 6 in (keel to planksheer). There is not much rise of floor but the bilges are well-rounded, and the waterlines are very fine-lined at each end. A small sail plan has raking masts and nothing set above royals, and this is confirmed by a painting of the ship reproduced in several Norwegian books. One trade for which fast ships were required in Norway was the carriage of fresh fruit which was particularly welcome in Baltic countries after a long winter. Schooners and brigantines were mostly employed here and some fine races were run, especially to St Petersburg after the ice melted.

In John Weale's series of books published in the last century, Hakon Sommerfeldt's *Construction of Ships* appeared in 1860, and the accompanying plates include a clipper ship 'to carry a load of 500 tons'. Although she has marked deadrise, the waterlines are not particularly sharp by British or American standards and she would only rate as a medium clipper. The proportions of the hull are those of a short, broad, but shallow-draft ship with a round stern and a foremast stepped right in the bows. On the sailplan, both the fore and main courses have vertical leeches; there are no skysails. The clipper had proportionally greater stability to carry a larger sail area than the 'common merchantman'. Comparing the two types, Sommerfeldt writes in the text:

'The clipper will ... have the disadvantage to require more men to work her, and her register tonnage will be greater, making the running expenses greater, and the cost of building her will be about 14% more than the cost of the common merchantman. Lastly, she will probably be more uneasy in a seaway. The clipper might have been made still sharper; but then all the disadvantages above mentioned would have been greater, and probably with heavy goods on board she might have been uneasy and run the risk to spring a leak and damage her cargo.'

This sums up well the reluctance many builders had for constructing really sharp vessels, and indicates why the softwood American clippers did not last too long when subjected to carrying guano, coal or other bulk cargoes. The incorporation of iron beams in British wooden ships undoubtedly helped to stiffen them and finally composite construction gave the best answer to the problem.

Denmark possessed many barques, brigs and barquentines in the China trade, and many of them remained in the Far East, trading along the China coast and between the various ports. Many were built to sail fast. Sailing out of Denmark, the barque *Svendborg* (1855 of 350 tons) is pictured as of clipper build with an Aberdeen-type bow.

At Apenrade in Denmark, Jörgen Bruhn built the large clipper *Cimber* in 1856 with dimensions of 237 ft 9 in (load waterline between perpendiculars) × 41 ft 0 in (moulded) × 22 ft 0 in (approx) and about 2,000 tons o.m. She had a long sharp entrance and an equally sharp run, but with more hollow worked in. The sail plan is not excessively large and there are no skysails; the sails on the mainmast do not overlap

The well-known clipper Noach, *which made some fast passages to and from the East Indies. She was built in 1857 at Kinderdijk. The yards appear to be fore-shortened here, unless lofty masts were intended to compensate for narrow yards.* (Prinz Hendrik Museum, Rotterdam).

those on other masts; and the courses have vertical leeches. She was celebrated for her passage of 106 days from Liverpool to San Francisco in 1856–57.

The design of clippers was carefully studied in Hamburg and Bremerhaven. At the latter port, the shipyard of R. C. Rickmers built *Ida Zeigler* (1854 of 955 tons) and *Augustus Wattenbach* (1855 of 1,575 tons) for the London-based firm of Wattenbach, Heilgers & Co; *Bellona* (1855 of 955 tons) for Rotterdam owners; *Melissa* (1853 of 648 tons) for Hamburg owners; and *Creole* (1856 of 437 tons) for themselves. A lines plan of *Ida Zeigler* traced by John Hilmann in about 1860 shows a long sharp vessel with a raking stem rabbet, and a lithograph pictures an even greater overhang to the stem. This lithograph suggests a large sail area with long lower yards, and shows two rows of reef points in the courses, three rows in the topsails and one row in the deep topgallants. She first traded with Calcutta, and then with New Zealand. At the Paris Exhibition of 1855, a model of the ship was awarded a medal, and R. C. Rickmers received a diploma signed by the Emperor Napoleon III himself.

At Altona, near Hamburg, Ernst Dreyer built several clippers, such as the barque *William O'Swald* (1854) which was their finest-lined clipper; also the ship *Imperieuse*

(1853) with a stem that raked forward with a big overhang, and the barque *Cid*, both for H. H. Eggers of Hamburg; and the ship *Esther* (1861) which was unusual in having a vertical stem like a fishing trawler, without a gammon knee or figurehead. In a paper on the *Development of Sailing Ship Construction in Hamburg and Altona*, Gerhard Timmermann writes that the 'cult of the clipper never existed in Germany'; and later, 'clipper ship construction, and with it the American influence, only played a very insignificant role in Germany'.

The lines and sail plan of an unidentified clipper of extreme model appeared in *Die Schiffbaukunst* by C. F. Steinhaus published in 1858. This clipper has a large sail plan, and the sails on the mainmast extensively overlap those on the fore and mizen; skysails could be set on each mast, and the yards on the foremast were the same length as those on the mainmast.

Several American clippers were owned in Hamburg such as the *Sovereign of the Seas*, as related in Chapter Five; Robert Sloman owned the *Electric* which was built at Mystic in 1854, and in 1869 he purchased the St John-built ship *Scottish Chief*. F. Roteus and D. H. Wätjen of Bremen also bought old American clippers. To the formation of the North German Federation in 1867 can be attributed the real start of the German merchant fleet.

It does not seem that the 'clipper cult' took hold in France to any great extent, although the carrying of prospectors and cargo to the Californian gold fields did fire the imagination, and many ships of all sizes and rigs cleared from French ports between 1850 and 1855. The fastest run was probably that made in 1853 by the *L'Alphonse-Nicolas Cézard* of 501 tons on the occasion of her second voyage. Under the command of Le Bozec, she sailed from Havre on 25 January and arrived at San Francisco on 15th May, 110 days later. When comparing this passage with those made from Boston or New York, one must not forget to deduct a week to account for the prevailing westerly winds encountered in beating out of the English Channel. On her first voyage, the ship had taken 122 days from Paimbeuf to San Francisco, sailing in October 1851.

French ships were also sailing direct to Australia during gold rush days and in 1853–54 the three masted schooner *Echo* of 212 tons took 111 days between Bordeaux and Melbourne. The fastest passage up to the middle of 1854 was probably that made by the *Fleur du Sud* which sailed from Havre to Melbourne in 90 days in 1853–54. She was becalmed on the 85th day when only 75 miles from Cape Otway. Of 471 tons, the *Melbourne Argus* described her as 'a fast sailing craft ... although not strictly a clipper', and that she was the first of a line to sail monthly between Havre and Melbourne.

The two principal builders of clippers were Arman of Bordeaux and Augustin Normand of Havre. The latter built the five sister ships *France et Chili, Paulista, Carioca, Petropolis*, and *Commerce de Paris* between 1850 and 1853. Admiral Paris reproduced a set of plans of these clippers in Volume 3 of *Souvenirs de Marine* with the result that mention of other French clippers is often ignored. The reason that these sister ships monopolize the subject is because no plans of other French clippers have been published. I used the plans in *Fast Sailing Ships*. The ships ran in the South American trade and *Paulista* of 609 tons once sailed from Chesapeake Bay to Rio de Janeiro in 30 days. As to hull-form, the entrance was short and sharp but the run was longer; there was considerable deadrise with rounded bilges and tumblehome, and a similar cross-section was later to be seen in the clippers *Leander* and *Thermopylae*. Other French clippers were the full-rigged ship *Saint-Pierre* built in 1856 at Havre of 830 tons, and *Imperatrice du Brésil*.

In 1866 there were only ten sailing ships owned in France that were built of iron, one of which was the *Carioca* built in 1866 at Nantes by E. Gouin & Co. of 791 tons. With a few exceptions, the construction of deep-water sailing ships of iron and steel was not adopted on the Continent of Europe until the day of the clipper was over, with the exception of Holland, where some fine iron clippers were built in the 1870s such as the *Industrie* of 1,846 tons built in 1872 by L. Smit at Kinderdijk and the *Batavier* of 1,780 tons built four years later by the same shipyard. Plans show them to have had flat floors with a short sharp entrance but a long hollow run. On deck, there was a tiny deck forward for working the anchors, a deckhouse abaft the foremast, and a raised quarter-deck aft. They were provided with a donkey boiler to raise steam to work the cargo winches and windlass. Composite construction also flourished in Holland for years.

The second Noach *was built ten years after the first one and was of 952 tons. This drawing shows a long poop reaching to the mainmast as well as a big deckhouse abaft the foremast. She continues the tradition of a lofty rig.* (Scheepvaart Museum, Amsterdam).

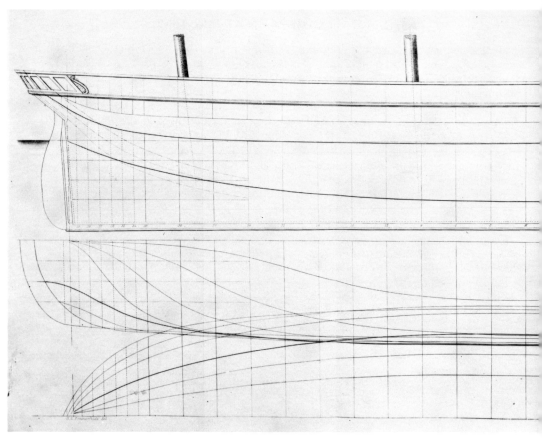

[**Above**] *'Draught of a Clipper Ship' from Sommerfeldt's book of plates published in 1860. She is a broad, short ship with fullish ends at bow and stern, although there is big deadrise.* (Author).

[**Right**] *The Danish barquentine* Nyborg *was built in 1866 of 284 tons and traded on the China coast and in Eastern waters. She was converted to a barge in 1907. The yards on the foremast are seen end-on which creates an odd impression.* (F. Holm-Petersen).

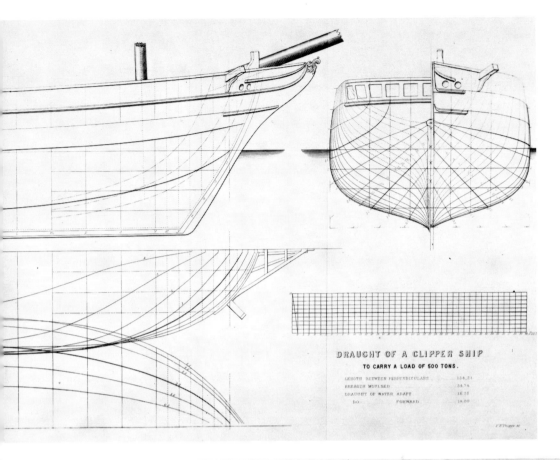

DRAUGHT OF A CLIPPER SHIP
TO CARRY A LOAD OF 500 TONS.

LENGTH BETWEEN PERPENDICULARS 134,71
BREADTH MOULDED 24,74
DRAUGHT OF WATER ABAFT 16,25
DO.   FORWARD 14,00

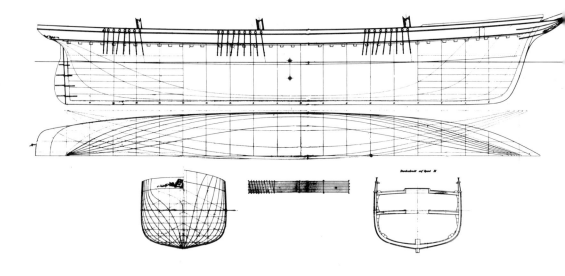

[**Below**] *A lithograph of an un-named French ship, having long lower and topsail yards, and setting nothing above her royals.* (Author).

[**Left**] *Lines plan of an unidentified clipper in* Die Schiffbaukunst *by C. F. Steinhaus, published in Hamburg in 1858, and therefore presumably of a German ship. Without much deadrise, the waterlines are extremely sharp.* (Author).

[**Below**] *A painting by J. Spin dated 1858, depicts the remarkably-rigged Dutch clipper* Argo *of 537 tons, built in 1854. As all her masts are 'two-piece' masts without any fidded topgallant masts, she could be called a four-masted schooner, especially as the fore and main lower masts are so long and set large gaff sails. Without the unusual jigger mast, the rig would have been similar to what is sometimes called a 'three-masted two-topsail schooner', which was found occasionally in Great Britain and northern Europe.* (Prinz Hendrik Museum, Rotterdam).

CHAPTER EIGHT

British Clippers of the 1860's

One result of the first clipper ship boom of 1853–55 was that most classes of British vessels were now built on somewhat finer lines than previously and the small loss of capacity caused by the finer lines at bow and stern was easily compensated by the increased length of the hulls. The slump of the late fifties was followed by a shipbuilding boom for both steam and sail tonnage in the first half of the sixties and a number of clippers were constructed. The increasing use of iron to reinforce wooden construction, as well as its adoption for entire hulls, produced very strong ships that could withstand the pressures of sail carrying as practised by some captains. In 1863, composite construction became popular for owners engaged in far eastern trades because the iron framework provided strength, but the external wooden planking permitted the use of copper sheathing and was also thought to cause less condensation in the hold. Such ships had long lives as the *Cutty Sark* can testify. So there were many clippers and medium clippers afloat in this decade but the extreme clippers were confined to the China tea trade.

William Rennie's design for the second *Fiery Cross* provides an example of a fast ship which was also the most successful China clipper in the years 1861 to 1865. This was a long period to be cock-of-the-walk with new clippers appearing every year, but Rennie could design a ship that could go to windward well and sail fast in light winds, and under the command of the energetic Richard Robinson it was an unbeatable combination. She won the premium as first ship home from China with the new teas on four occasions, while three of her outward passages to Hong Kong or Shanghai against the north-east monsoon averaged 90 days. She was of 695 tons with dimensions of 185.0 ft × 31.7 ft × 19.2 ft and was built in 1860 at Liverpool by Chaloner. She could carry 1,050 tons of tea.

William Rennie also designed the clippers *Black Prince*, *John R. Worcester* and *Norman Court*, and the auxiliary steamer *Sea King* which later became the confederate raider *Shenandoah*.

Fiery Cross possessed very sharp lines with appreciable rise of floor which was accentuated by the hollow garboards which increased the apparent depth of the keel.

Another clipper built in 1860 was the *Flying Spur* of 732 tons which came from Alexander Hall's yard at Aberdeen and she was commanded by John Ryrie, late master of the *Cairngorm*. Frederick Paton, who was a midshipman in her from 1865–70, wrote of her as 'a very fast vessel, as good as the fastest I should say, with the exception perhaps of the *Ariel* and *Spindrift*'. He inferred that as Ryrie was a part-owner of *Flying Spur*, he did not drive the ship in strong winds but 'nursed her'. Nevertheless she

The small 258-ton barque Prince Alfred *ready for launching from Duthie's yard at Aberdeen in 1862. The new black paint glistens and below it the copper sheathing looks like a stone wall. She traded with Natal.* (J. Henderson).

performed some fast passages and did make 328 miles on one occasion in 24 hours, and once made the passage to Sydney in 73 days. In a letter to Basil Lubbock, written in 1910, Paton described how *Flying Spur* passed another ship:

'I remember once when coming home with the 1st Season's tea, we had just got the NE trades strong and were bowling along at 13 knots with all sail set that she would bear, including royal staysails, the lower yards just touching the backstays, when at 11.20 am we sighted a sail ahead, perhaps 12 miles off. Well, soon after 1 pm we passed her, she hoisting her signals asking us to report her at Lloyd's. She was the Glasgow clipper ship *Lochleven Castle*, 80 days out from Rangoon bound to Liverpool. As we passed her our lee rails were under water; also the cook was washed out of the galley to the break of the half poop with all his pots and pans. The main topgallant sail of the *Lochleven Castle* went to ribbons about that time, and her mainsail split so badly that they hauled it up. She was out of sight in an hour and a half.'

This sounds as if Captain Ryrie could drive his ship along if he wanted to do so.

Various clippers were built in the next two years such as *Ganges* (1861 of iron by William Pile), *Min* (1861 of wood by Robert Steele), *Mansfield* (1861 by Benjamin Nicholson) and *Coulnakyle* (1862 by Alexander Hall). But with the reduction of duties of imported tea falling from 1s 5d (7p) to 1s 0d (5p) per pound in 1863 and then halving two years later, orders were placed for a new range of tea clippers and this resulted in the celebrated productions from the Greenock yard of Robert Steele & Co. Beginning in 1863 with *Serica* and *Taeping*, the fastest clippers from this builder continued with *Ariel* and *Sir Lancelot* in 1865, and *Titania*, *Lahloo*, *Kaisow* and *Wylo* in successive years. *Serica* was of wood but the rest were of composite construction, and they seem to have set the standard by which to judge the other tea clippers.

Many fine ships were launched from British yards in 1863, the pick of the bunch being *Black Prince* which was said to have been an improvement on *Fiery Cross*; *Coonatto*; *Eliza Shaw*; *Wild Deer*, which was Charles Connell's first composite ship; *Taeping* and *Serica*. In spite of her hard-driving master, Innes, and her sharper hull, *Serica* was often beaten by *Taeping* on the homeward run from China. On her maiden passage with tea, *Taeping* was dismasted off Amoy in July 1864, but after refitting she came home in only 88 days to Deal with the north-east monsoon in her favour. *Serica* won the premium as the first ship home in 1864, just beating the *Fiery Cross* by one day.

These ships were beautifully equipped with deck fittings made of varnished teak and much brasswork to be polished; the bowsprit, lower masts, topmasts and their yards were now made of tubular iron or steel for sufficient strength, but the other spars were of wood. The ships were fully equipped with stunsails and *Flying Spur* used to set fourteen of them. All ships had a graceful bow terminating in a figurehead supported by the traditional carved trail boards, with sides quite smooth, unlike the rough scarred sides of the *Cutty Sark* today, and with no forecastle or poop to spoil the line of the sheer. There was a big deckhouse abaft the foremast, and the after accommodation was in a raised quarter-deck, half of which was sunk into the upper deck. An occasional clipper was painted white, some had green hulls, but the majority were black. Inboard, the bulwarks were often covered with painted floral panels that were sometimes stowed safely away before the ship proceeded to sea.

In 1864, Alexander Stephen & Sons of Glasgow built the *Mofussilite* at a cost of £20.50 per ton in composite construction. This shipbuilder had several enquiries to build tea clippers from the very owners who finally ordered from Robert Steele, but his prices must have been higher or he would have got the job. After the extreme iron clippers which he launched in the 1850s, he never built another full-blooded clipper of any note, although he built numerous medium clippers for the China and far eastern trades. Alexander Stephen Jnr was probably the man most responsible for getting composite construction adopted, as he pushed Lloyd's Register hard to obtain a classification equal to a wooden ship, and he visited many owners quoting prices and telling them the advantages of this construction. Unfortunately it was much more expensive than a hull composed of nothing but iron. The medium clippers *William Davie* (1865) or *Norham Castle* (1869) were probably his finest-lined ships of the sixties.

Perhaps the clipper *par excellence*, the ship against which most seamen wanted to try their paces, was the lovely *Ariel*, launched in 1865 by Robert Steele & Co, to the order of Shaw, Lowther & Maxton of London. Her measurements were 197.4 ft × 33.9 ft × 21.0 ft and 853 tons. She was a flush-decked ship, with a small anchor deck forward, a small deckhouse abaft the foremast, but no poop or raised quarter-deck. In conditions when her master, John Keay, wrote in his journal: 'Ship plunging heavily whole lee bow and lee quarter under water alternately' (18th June 1867) there would not have been a dry place anywhere on deck.

It has been contended that *Ariel* was exceptionally fine aft and lacked bearing in the quarters and that this accounted for her being posted missing in 1872. But the builder's plans do not make her any finer here than other clippers unless the lines were altered on the mould loft floor. She was certainly a very fine-lined clipper with a long entrance and run, and marked rise of floor. The *Sir Lancelot*, built for the rival firm of J. MacCunn, had the same set of lines as *Ariel*, according to the builder's plan, which is a strange circumstance when the blue riband of the China trade, namely the homeward passage from Foochow, was at stake. This fact lends additional support to the contention that one or both of the clippers were altered in the mould loft. Both were of composite construction and probably cost about £18 per ton. *Sir Lancelot* was not flush-decked, but had a conventional deck layout. As to the sail plan, *Ariel* carried double topsails on each mast and three headsails; *Sir Lancelot* had double topsails on fore and main masts but a single topsail on the mizen, and she had four headsails. Both set a main skysail and every possible flying kite.

Captain John Keay had *Ariel* for three voyages: on the first she had the world famous race home with *Taeping* and *Serica*, generally referred to as the 'Great Tea Race'; on her second voyage she broke the record by sailing out to Hong Kong from London against the monsoon in 83 days or in only 79 days 21 hours between her pilots, 17th October to 5th January 1866–67. Ships like her could command freights of between 10s (50p) and £1 per ton higher than lesser ships.

But to return to the passage home in 1866. The first five ships crossed Foochow bar in the following order: *Fiery Cross* (29th May); *Ariel, Serica* and *Taeping* (30th May); *Taitsing* (31st May). *Ariel* loaded 1,230,900 lbs of tea at £5 per ton and her bills of lading were endorsed for '10s per ton extra if first sailing vessel in dock with new teas from Foochow'. *Fiery Cross* passed Anjer one day ahead of the other four and once logged 328 miles when crossing the Indian Ocean. But somehow she dropped behind after passing Flores in the Azores on the same day as *Ariel, Taeping* and *Serica*, because she did not pass Deal until over 24 hours after these three. The excitement felt all over the country when the story was recounted of how *Ariel* and *Taeping* sailed up the

Clippers waiting to load tea at Foochow in 1866. From left to right the names given on the photograph are: Black Prince, Fiery Cross, Taeping, Ariel *and* Flying Spur. Taeping *and* Ariel *are probably interchanged, but even then,* Ariel *should have a skysail mast on the main, which this ship does not.* Fiery Cross, *according to a painting, did experiment with double topsails on the mainmast only.* (Peabody Museum of Salem).

English Channel almost side by side throughout the fifth of September, often logging 14 knots, is vividly recaptured by Frederick Paton:

'The *Ariel*'s captain thought he was a long way ahead of any other ship, and had taken down all his studding sail booms, but when off the Lizard at daylight in the morning, saw the *Taeping* close under the quarter, he then had most of the studding sails set once more and the two ships raced up Channel. They were very evenly matched so that they took pilots and tugs almost at the same time. The *Serica* came up Channel along the French coast and did not see either of the other two ships, but she also got her pilot soon after they did their's, and docked the same tide, but an hour or so later.'

Ariel actually signalled her number off Deal at 8 am on 6th September 1866, 98 days $22\frac{1}{2}$ hours after dropping her pilot off Foochow; *Taeping* got there ten minutes later. The premium was divided but was discontinued in future years. Prices of tea fell on the market with so many clippers arriving simultaneously which was a deplorable thing, from the tea dealers' point of view.

Of other tea clippers built in 1865, *Taitsing*, which was built at Glasgow by Connell, has already been mentioned; there was also *Maitland* built by William Pile at Sunderland for J. R. Kelso who owned numerous clippers such as *Kelso* (1861), *Undine* (1867) and *Deerhound* (1869). The *Maitland* was celebrated for setting moonsails above her skysails.

Many ships sailed outwards to Australia, crossed over to China and returned home with tea to London, but others hardly ever deviated from the Australian trade. The Orient Line had some fine composite clippers in the sixties which concentrated on the trade with Adelaide, such as *The Goolwa* (1864 by A. Hall), *Yatala* (1865 by Bilbe & Perry) and *Argonaut* (1866 by Bilbe & Perry). The *Yatala* once went from London to Adelaide in 65 days between her pilots, a record which she shared with *City of Adelaide*. The latter still lies in Glasgow as the RNVR club ship disguised under the name of *Carrick*. She was built in 1864 by William Pile of 791 tons, and forms a remarkable survival from this byegone era. Also dating from 1864 was the *John Duthie* which was one of a number of big wooden medium clippers which the Aberdeen shipbuilder Duthie & Sons, launched annually. They usually were in the 900 to 1,100 tons range and were lofty ships setting skysails on each mast.

Another Aberdeen shipyard, Walter Hood & Co, built regularly for George Thompson's 'White Star Line' such ships as *Queen of Nations* (1861), *Ethiopian* (1864), *Harlaw* (1866), *Thyatira* (1867), *Thermopylae* (1868) and *Patriarch* (1869). All these ships had green-painted hulls with white masts and yards, and looked very smart. *Harlaw* made some fast passages from China with the favourable north-east monsoon such as 87 days from Shanghai to New York in 1872.

Captain Richard Robinson left the *Fiery Cross* to take command of the *Sir Lancelot* on her second voyage and made her one of the fastest China clippers. Her maiden passage under McDougall had been a disaster and the second passage began most inauspiciously as the clipper was completely dismasted on 13th December 1866 off Ushant. She was hastily re-rigged at Falmouth in six weeks with Oregon pine masts, during severe winter weather. But Robinson soon left his mark on the clipper. Homeward bound in 1867, she encountered *Flying Spur* off the Cape of Good Hope, and Frederick Paton who was a midshipman on the latter, described their meeting, when writing to Basil Lubbock:

'It was a stormy day, and we were carrying what was thought by us to be a heavy press of sail, viz, whole topsails and courses with outer jib, whilst other ships in

The Electra *was a regular trader to New Zealand under the ownership of Shaw, Savill & Co. She was built in 1866 at Aberdeen by A. Hall & Sons. She was a typical example of one of Hall's medium clippers of the sixties.* (Alexander Turnbull Library).

company were close-reefed; when we sighted a clipper ship on the other tack carrying three topgallant sails and flying jib. This was an enormous amount of sail considering the wind, and she would not have possibly done so but the swell was running abaft her beam, whilst it was right ahead with us.

'Well, we were of course anxious to know the name of that ship and as soon as she got near enough, we began signalling. She proved to be the *Sir Lancelot* from Hankow, Capt. Robinson, who had previously commanded the *Fiery Cross.* She crossed our bows and just then when the signalling was going on, her helmsman, paying too much attention to us, allowed her to come up in the wind and get aback. We thought that she would have been dismasted, she heeling right over and getting sternway. However, they managed to get some sail off her and she righted, but it was a close thing.

'As the ships were fairly close, we could see all that took place on board of her. We saw Capt. Robinson knock down the man at the wheel and jump on him! After that, we were in company for some days, the ships being of the same speed.'

The *Flying Spur* had a crew of 36 all told: master, 3 officers, 2 midshipmen, 20 able seamen, 2 ordinary seamen, carpenter, joiner, boatswain, sailmaker, cook, 2 stewards and a butcher. Paton thought this 'a big crew for a vessel of 735 tons register, but then of course she was very heavily rigged'. Clippers could only carry so much canvas by having permanent iron ballast in the bottom of their holds.

The fastest tea clipper to be launched in 1866 was the *Titania*, which was built by Steele of Greenock for the same owners as *Ariel*. She was some $2\frac{1}{2}$ ft longer, also 2 ft broader, but of similar depth. She had much greater rise of floor and was somewhat finer in the entrance and run, making her an extreme clipper. Like the *Ariel* she was also flush-decked with a similar sail plan. When her spars were shortened in the seventies for the sake of economy, it was probably then that two large deckhouses were erected for her crew and officers in order to increase her stowage capacity previously occupied by the men. This may have happened to *Ariel* also, because a much-reproduced oil painting shows these two houses.

It was often difficult for shipowners to secure the right master who could handle such a ticklish ship to perfection, and *Titania's* first master, Robert Deas, while entirely competent, could not get the best out of her. But under Captains Burgoyne and Dowdy she really began to move. In 1869 she was only 96 days between Woosung and Deal, having sailed against the monsoon.

Another ship built in 1866 was the *Sobraon* which was the largest composite-built ship ever constructed in Great Britain, measuring 272.0 ft × 40.0 ft × 27.0 ft and 2,131 tons net register. She was produced by Alexander Hall & Sons for Gellatly, Hankey & Sewell at a cost of £43,965, having been designed as an auxiliary steamer, but this idea was abandoned during construction and the screw aperture filled in. This resulted in a long run which, combined with a fine entrance, made her a fast clipper. However as a ship carrying passengers on two decks, she was never driven hard out of consideration to them and her best day's work was only 340 miles, although 16 knots were regularly achieved. Her life was spent entirely in the Australian trade and in 1891 she was sold to the New South Wales Government for a reformatory, being gradually rigged down over the years. She was not broken up until 1941. Her fastest passage out to Sydney was 73 days; to Melbourne it was 68 days. She was always a very popular ship with both passengers and crew.

It is curious how there was a rush to build clipper ships as the sixties drew to their close, in spite of the steady increase in the number of steamers being launched and their greater efficiency. The Suez Canal was under construction but obviously shipowners thought there was still some money to be made. Shipbuilding costs had certainly not risen; if anythng they were tending to edge downwards, but then so were freights from China, and only an exceptional clipper could load at £5 per ton. Most loaded at £4 per ton or less.

On the evidence of plans and models, five extreme clippers still remained to be launched in the sixties: *Spindrift* and *Leander* in 1867, *Thermopylae* in 1868, *Cutty Sark* and *The Caliph* in 1869.

The extreme clipper *Spindrift* had a short life, being wrecked at Dungeness at the start of her third voyage in November 1869. She was built by Charles Connell at Glasgow in 1867 for James Findlay, who already owned *Serica* and *Taitsing*. She had great rise of floor with a big tumblehome, and her waterlines were very sharp so that although her tonnage was 892 she cannot have carried much more than a thousand tons of cargo. Her fastest passage was 96 days from Foochow to London in 1868.

Another extreme clipper built at Glasgow in the same year was the *Leander*, designed by Bernard Waymouth and constructed by J. G. Lawrie. She was very fine-lined with great deadrise and very rounded bilges, but was a wet ship under a press of sail when loaded down to her marks. She had a large sail plan with very deep topgallant sails but no skysails; there were double topsails on fore and main masts and a single mizen topsail; the main topgallant sail was fitted with Colling & Pinkney's roller-reefing gear. *Thermopylae* embodied all these features in her own sail plan, except that she carried double topsails on all three masts.

Launched the following year from Walter Hood & Co's yard at Aberdeen, the green-hulled *Thermopylae* was also designed by Waymouth and measured 212.0 ft × 36.0 ft × 20.9 ft and 948 tons net. She closely resembled *Leander* in hull-form, but although $3\frac{1}{2}$ ft shorter, about 1 ft broader and of the same depth of hold, *Thermopylae*'s under deck tonnage was 927 as against 848. She may have been a little fuller somewhere in her hull, and if so, it was probably in the quarters under her counter. At any rate, *Thermopylae* could be driven much harder in strong winds, carried more cargo and certainly was not slower under sail. In fact, under Kemball, she was remarkably fast and her maiden voyage was talked about in ships' foc'sles for many years, while her track at sea and her abstract log were pasted into many private journals.

On this famous maiden voyage, she passed the Lizard on 8 November 1868 and sighted Cape Otway 60 days later on 7 January 1869, while the time from Gravesend to Hobson's Bay, Melbourne, was only 63 days.

Up to this date the record had been held by the huge clipper *James Baines* which had taken 63 days from Rock Light or 64 days from Liverpool to Melbourne in 1854–55. *Thermopylae* then went round to Newcastle, and from there was only 31 days to Shanghai, or 28 days between her pilots, again setting up a new record.

While waiting to load tea at Foochow, she displayed a gilded cock at her main truck in witness of her speed. This was too much for the crews of the other ships because *Thermopylae* still had to prove her mettle on the homeward race, and one night, so the story goes, a seaman from the *Taeping* swam across to the green clipper, climbed aloft unseen and made off with the trophy. In due course the cock was replaced.

But *Thermopylae* did prove her worth by only taking 89 days to the Lizard which she passed on 30 September or 91 days to London. This entire voyage was a remarkable performance and has never been equalled before or since. But to Captain Kemball's chagrin, his record run from Foochow was eclipsed by two days, only a fortnight later, when the *Sir Lancelot* under Richard Robinson passed the Lizard on 10 October a mere 84 days after leaving the River Min, her total time from Foochow to dock in London being 89 days, from 17 July to 13 October. This is certainly the fastest passage made from China when sailing against the monsoon. A table of other record passages is given in the Appendix.

Most of George Thompson's ships combined the Australian and China trades. *Thermopylae*'s first ten outward passages, all made to Melbourne, averaged 69 days from the Lizard, and her eleven tea-laden passages averaged $106\frac{1}{2}$ days. Many captains were content to have made a single passage equalling one of these averages in a complete lifetime at sea!

Some other fine clippers had been built for the China trade in 1867 including *Undine* built by Pile for J. R. Kelso, *Lahloo* built by Steele for A. Rodger, and *Derwent* built by Barclay, Curle & Co as a three-masted barque; Alexander Hall & Sons launched the ship *Nicova* for the Costa Rica coffee trade.

[**Above**] *Alexander Hall & Sons' Yard at Aberdeen in 1862, with members of the Hall family and their principal tradesmen. The ships in frame are the* Coulnakyle *(left) and* Natal Star. *The former was a tea clipper of 579 tons.* (J. Henderson).

[**Opposite**] *It is probably from 1863 that Robert Steele's tea clippers first began to achieve fame, and in that year he launched two lovely clippers: the* Taeping, *seen here, and* Serica. *In this lithograph by T. G. Dutton,* Taeping *does not have her main skysail yard crossed.* (Parker Gallery).

Clippers were sliding down the ways throughout the following year. On the Clyde, Robert Steele produced another beauty called *Kaisow* and named after one of the China teas; she was built for A. Rodger and in 1875 came under the ownership of Killick, Martin & Co. *Wylo*, which Killick ordered from Steele the following year, had almost identical dimensions, and so they were probably sister ships. Connell built the *City of Perth* later renamed *Turakina* for the New Zealand trade. At Aberdeen, Alexander Hall & Sons built the powerful *Herradura* which was designed to round Cape Horn for the Costa Rica coffee trade; they also launched the small 200-ton barque *Samoa* for the London Missionary Society, who renamed her *John Williams* before she began her maiden voyage. Her plans appeared in *Fast Sailing Ships*, Fig. 266.

Although steamers were being ordered by the very shipowners who possessed some of the fleetest clippers afloat, not less than 132 ocean-going sailing ships were launched in the very year that the Suez Canal was finally opened, namely in 1869. Out of all these ships, the two most extreme clippers were *Cutty Sark* and *The Caliph*, although *Norman Court* was almost as sharp. Killick, Martin & Co added three new vessels to their fleet: the full-rigged ship *Wylo*, and two small barques built by Pile, the *Miako* and *Osaka*. William Pile also built the *Deerhound*; Walker launched the *Ambassador* into the Thames at Rotherhithe; on the Clyde, Connell completed the *Eme* and *Duke of Abercorn*. All these ships were built for the China trade, now becoming over-stocked with clippers and racing steamers.

Of all the names listed above, the *Cutty Sark* is today the best known because she has survived and is preserved in dry dock at Greenwich under the watchful eye of the *Cutty Sark* Society. It is a curious fact that the British merchant marine in the days of sail should be represented by one of the extreme clippers which comprised a mere fraction of the countless ships afloat, rather than by a more typical medium clipper or bluff-bowed cargo carrier. The clippers certainly embodied the highest standards in their design and equipment, and the strength of her composite construction has helped the *Cutty Sark*'s survival. Of course, Captain Dowman appeared at just the right time to ensure that the Portuguese did not break her up and he restored her at Falmouth in the 1920s. She was brought round to the Thames in 1938.

Like most ships, *Cutty Sark* has had an eventful career which began with her builders, Scott & Linton of Dumbarton, going bankrupt, and her being completed by the neighbouring yard of Denny Bros. She was ordered by John Willis of London at a cost of £21 per ton, with dimensions of 212.5 ft × 36.0 ft × 21.0 ft and 921 tons net. She had a large sail area with a main yard measuring 78 ft long. She was designed by Hercules Linton with a very sharp-ended hull and big deadrise, and she could beat the other tea clippers in strong winds. Her maximum speed was $17\frac{1}{2}$ knots giving a speed–length ratio of 1.20. Her coefficient of under deck tonnage is .55, which is the same as *Crest of the Wave* and *Hallowe'en*, but .03 less than *Thermopylae*.

Perhaps *Cutty Sark* never made a passage home from China in less than 100 days because she did not have a skipper with sufficient drive and daring. But later, when carrying wool home from Australia, the reverse was the case under Woodget, and she made many fast runs such as 69 days from Newcastle, NSW, to the Lizard in 1887–88, and 70 days to the Lizard from Sydney on the previous voyage. On these passages she met her old rival *Thermopylae*, but now the tables were turned as *Cutty Sark* excelled in the strong winds met with in the southern latitudes.

After he retired from the sea, Captain Woodget ran the coal importing business at Overy Staithe on the north Norfolk coast, and when Basil Lubbock was collecting material for his book, *Log of the 'Cutty Sark'*, he had to follow Woodget about, listening to his yarns of clipper ship days, as the old man milked the goats or tended the coal-laden schooners.

Of the other clippers built for the China trade in 1869, *The Caliph* was produced by Alexander Hall & Sons as a very fine-lined ship with considerable deadrise, and was very heavily sparred with many flying kites. But she made only one complete voyage, on the return part of which she took 87 days between Foochow and New York in 1870–71. Returning to China from London, she was posted missing after passing Anjer on 15th August 1871.

William Rennie's last clipper design was the *Norman Court* of 884 tons, ordered by Baring Brothers of London and built on the Clyde. She excelled at going to windward and was fast in light winds. Andrew Shewan, the younger, was master for six years from 1873 and has left many memories of her which were published in his book *The Great Age of Sail*. But in an old volume of the magazine *Sea Breezes*, he writes of her:

'Though so staunch and tight, yet at times the whole fabric would tremble like a piece of whalebone. When we were driving her into a head sea, I have noted, as I lay on the after lockers, that after a heavy plunge as she recovered herself the after end would vibrate like a diving board when the pressure is released.'

Some fine ships were built for the Australian trade in 1869 such as the *Beltana*, the barque-rigged *Berean*—both of composite construction—and the iron-hulled ships *Patriarch*, *Thomas Stephens*, *Loch Ness* and *Loch Tay*. Constructed by Walter Hood &

At Port Adelaide in 1867, the Pekina *(left) and* Coonatto *are discharging cargo, using their main yards as cranes.* Pekina *was built at Aberdeen by Smith in 1865 and has Colling & Pinkney's roller reefing topsails.* Coonatto *was built in 1863 at London by Bilbe & Perry, and made some fast passages under Captain Begg.* (Arthur D. Edwardes).

Co's yard at Aberdeen for George Thompson's 'White Star Line', the *Patriarch* was Thompson's first iron ship, measuring 221.1 ft × 38.1 ft × 22.3 ft and 1,339 tons, and she cost some £24,000. She was unique in that her lower and topmasts were of tubular iron in one length without any doubling, and the topgallant masts were telescopic and slid inside the topmasts. Although the *Star of Bengal* and *Star of Russia*, both built in 1874, had their lower masts and topmasts in one continuous piece, their topgallant masts were fidded in the usual manner, and *Patriarch*'s style of masting was not repeated in other ships. The iron clipper *Hurricane*, built by Alexander Stephen & Sons in 1853, had a sail plan drawn in *Patriarch*'s manner, but she does not appear to have been rigged accordingly. The *Patriarch*'s maiden voyage in 1869–70 was a record one as she was only 67 days pilot to pilot from London to Sydney and homeward-bound she took 69 days from Sydney Heads to the dock in London.

Lovers of sail can take comfort in the fact that as a result of the race to Sydney and back made in 1975–76 by ocean racing yachts, backed up by all the techniques and weather lore which twentieth century radio and science can devise, the 77 ft ketch *Great Britain II* only managed to short cut *Patriarch*'s times by 41 hours on the outward trip and just under 50 hours for the homeward passage. The types of craft pitted against each other are so disproportionate that any rational comparison is impossible.

[**Opposite top**] *The* Wild Deer, *seen here in dry dock at Port Chalmers, was originally a tea clipper, but after 1871 was in the New Zealand trade. Of 1016 tons, the stern carving was typical of many ships.* (Alexander Turnbull Library).

[**Opposite bottom**] *This group on the bows of the* Wild Deer *fixes the scale of the parts which together form the features that make up the traditional shape of a clipper, but the fairly crude details are sometimes overlooked. The carving, figurehead and trailboards had to withstand the battering of seas and the buffeting in harbour.* (Alexander Turnbull Library).

[**Below**] *Sail plan of the medium clipper* Northam Castle *which was built by Alexander Stephen & Sons at Glasgow in 1869; she was of 698 tons and had a length of 177.4 ft. She has a typical sail plan for ships of under a thousand tons during the sixties.* (Author).

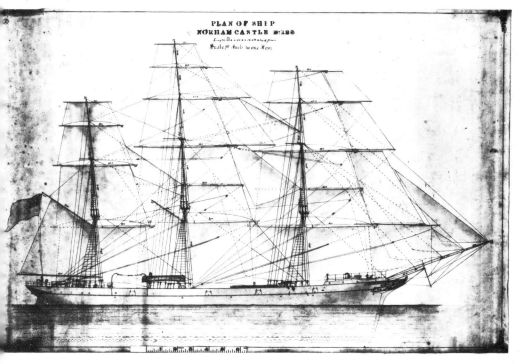

[**Above**] *This oil painting of the* Ariel *is by W. B. Spencer and shows her as a flush-decked ship without a poop or quarter deck; she is under a press of sail up to royal stunsails, although it is curious to note that the main skysail yard is not even crossed.* (Parker Gallery).

[**Opposite**] *This model of the* Taitsing *shows the relation of hull to masts and rigging. With the exception of the main skysail, the sail outlines would be the same as on the* Norham Castle. *She was built by Connell of Glasgow in 1865 who two years earlier launched the* Wild Deer, *bow and stern views of which are reproduced here.* (Glasgow Art Gallery and Museum).

[**Right**] *Bows of the* Carrick *photographed in 1951 on the Clyde. She is still used as an R.N.V.R. Club ship but her future is uncertain. As the last clipper ship still afloat, she is in urgent need of a sponsor. She was built in 1864 at Sunderland by William Pile with the name* City of Adelaide. (Author).

[**Above**] *At anchor in Durban harbour, the* Umgeni *has hoisted her sails to dry in the hot sun. She was a small full-rigged ship of 366 tons, built at Aberdeen by 'Yankee' Smith in 1864. The jibs and staysails look especially large.* (Local History Museum, Durban).

[**Opposite**] *The shapely bows of the* Sobraon, *when the ship was drydocked in Sutherland Dock, Cockatoo Island, Sydney, in 1891. She was built at Aberdeen in 1866 of 2130 tons and had spent all her life trading between London and Australia. The hull was planked with wood on iron frames.* (C. L. Hume).

[**Below**] *Lying in the sound at Esquimalt, British Columbia, in about 1890, is the tea clipper* Titania. *Built in 1866 by Robert Steele & Co. on extremely sharp lines, she began life with an open flush deck like the* Ariel, *but two large deckhouses were later added, as shown in this photograph.* (Provincial Archives, Victoria, B.C.).

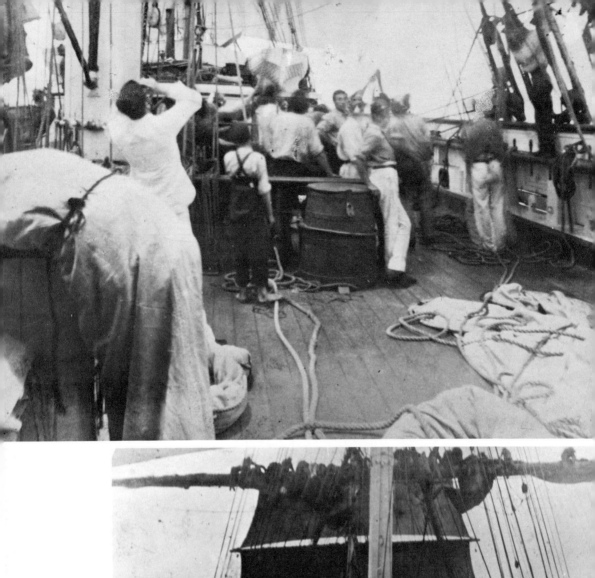

Scenes aboard the Sobraon.
[**Above**] *Apprentices washing down the decks.*

[**Opposite top**] *Changing sails, with the crew standing at the foot of the mainmast; a sail is lying on the deck at right; another is on the left.*

[**Opposite bottom**] *A wet stormy day, with the watch on the main yard, furling the sail.*

[**Right**] *The petty officers pose with their tools in their hands: in front is the boiler man known as 'engines' with a hammer; on the left is the bosun with a marline spike; on the right is the sailmaker, called 'sails', with his 'palm'; standing is 'chips', the carpenter, with a mallet.* (Author).

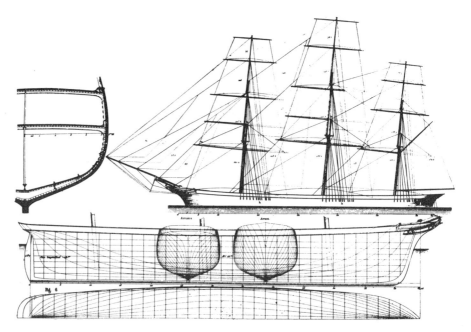

[**Left**] *Sail plan and lines plan of the extreme clipper* Leander, *built at Glasgow in 1867 from a design by Bernard Waymouth. She had dimensions of 210.0 ft × 35.2 ft × 20.8 ft and 883 tons.* Thermopylae, *launched the following year, was of almost similar hull-form.* (L'Art Naval ... Jusqu'en 1869 *by Adml. Paris*).

[**Below right**] *Painted white and reduced to a barque, nothing could disguise the beautiful lines of* Thermopylae, *seen here at Bullins Way, Esquimalt, British Columbia, in about 1895, when trading across the Pacific under Canadian ownership.* (Provincial Archives, Victoria, B.C.).

[**Below left**] *Two tea clippers lying in the River Min at Foochow. The photograph ascribes the date to 1868 and the ships as* Sir Lancelot *(left) and* Spindrift. *But the latter two did not look like this. Instead, the most likely candidates are* Ariel *(left) and* Thermopylae, *and the year 1869. I have reconstructed the rigging above the top of the hills where it had been printed out.* (Peabody Museum of Salem).

[**Above**] *Robert Steele's last tea clipper was the* Wylo, *painted by a Chinese artist, and bearing Killick, Martin & Co's houseflag. She was built in 1869.* (Killick, Martin & Co Ltd).

[**Below**] *On a slip in Table Bay, Cape Town, the* Crusader *has been stripped down to her lower masts, with the topmasts 'housed', to carry out repairs — presumably major ones. This barque was built in 1863 at Sunderland by Robinson; she was of 334 tons and measured 108.0 ft × 26.5 ft × 16.7 ft.* (Elliott Collection, Cape Archives, South Africa).

With a list to port, the Ferreira *ex* Cutty Sark *lies at Muscogee Wharf, Pensacola, on 27 September 1906, after a hurricane had swept the town. The fore royal mast and its yard are hanging in the topgallant rigging.* Cutty Sark *had been sold to Portuguese owners who had previously renamed her. The dolphin striker is broken at its lower end and the chain stays leading to it are slack.* (Smithsonian Institution).

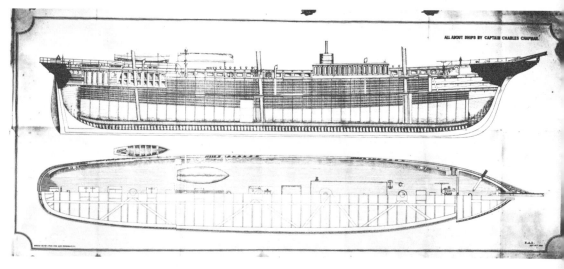

ALL ABOUT SHIPS BY CAPTAIN CHARLES CHAPMAN

[**Above**] *Longitudinal section through the hold of the extreme clipper* The Caliph, *and below it the plan of the main deck. This deck is bisected to show the deck fittings (above) and the iron beams (below).* (Author).

[**Above**] *Aboard the* Patriarch, '*screwing*' *wool. The stevedores are trying to force the last bales into the hold through the main hatch. The mainmast is on the left.* (C. L. Hume).

[**Left**] *The Australian clipper* Houghton Tower, *built in 1869 at Birkenhead by Clover and of 1598 tons. Her maiden passage took 75 days between Liverpool and Melbourne. She was a handsome ship with a large spread of sail.* (Mariners Museum, Newport News).

[**Above**] *The iron-hulled clipper* Patriarch *under sail off Sydney Heads in the 1890's. This ship was built in 1869 with a length of 221 ft. The yards have been hauled round to brace the ship up on the port tack, but the royals are not set nor their yards braced round.* (The late A. D. Edwardes).

[**Opposite**] *A splendid action shot of the* Golden Fleece *running into Le Havre with a following wind. Of 1257 tons, she was built of iron in 1869 for Carmichael's 'Golden Fleece' Line; all his ships were named after characters in this Greek legend.* (A. J. Nesdall).

[**Below**] *A century after she was launched, the wooden planking has been stripped off the iron frames of the* Ambassador *where she lies at Punta Arenas, Magellan Straits. This ship of 692 tons was built on the Thames at Rotherhithe in 1869.* (Alan Villiers).

CHAPTER NINE

American Clippers after 1860

At the commencement of the Civil War in 1860, the total tonnage registered in America of both sailing vessels and steamers exceeded that registered in Great Britain for the same categories, the figures being 5,299,000 as against 4,659,000 tons. But the Civil War curtailed the building of deep water sailing ships so that by 1870 American tonnage had declined to 4,195,000 tons whereas British tonnage had risen to 5,691,000 for both sail and steam. Neither did the building of clipper ships ever approach anything on the scale of the boom in the first half of the fifties, and nor did it emulate in any way the boom for building clippers in the sixties which Great Britain enjoyed. On the other hand, some splendid medium clippers were constructed in the 'Down East' states of Maine, New Hampshire, Massachusetts and Connecticut.

British shipbuilders were turning rapidly to the use of iron for hulls as the import of timber was costly when coal and iron ore deposits were on their doorstep. But the forests of America were ready to supply the shipyards with all the timber needed, and very few square-riggers were ever built of iron or steel. American shipowners were busy selling their worn out clippers to British and Continental owners during the war years and few clippers of the fifties survived into the seventies. The best known survivors were the *Syren* and *N. B. Palmer* (both 1851), *Malay* (1852), *Young America*, *Great Republic*, *Dashing Wave* and *David Crockett* (all built 1853), *Wild Hunter* and *War Hawk* (both 1855), and *Prima Donna* (1858).

The Australian trade proved attractive for American ships just as it did for the British, but the growing export of wheat from San Francisco to Europe drew ships of all nationalities and once again American medium clippers were rounding Cape Horn for California, just as they had done in gold-rush days.

Built as they were in the 'Down East' states these medium clippers became known as 'Down-Easters'. In hull-form they had a moderately fine entrance but a longer and finer run; to carry the maximum amount of cargo, they were full-bodied amidships with almost flat floors which were carried fore and aft. This form of hull gave great power to carry sail and enabled them to make passages which were sometimes as fast as those made by the clippers of the 1850s. Although they did not carry the numerous flying kites of the earlier clippers, many of these Down-Easters carried stunsails on the foremast as well as skysails on each mast. With one or two exceptions, the hulls were given little ornamentation and no trail boards to support the figurehead. Hulls were nearly always painted black but the cotton canvas was whiter than flax canvas. By British standards, they were huge for wooden ships, 1,500 tons being a fair average. This form of medium clipper continued to be built until the mid-eighties, culminating

The full rigged ship Independence *under full sail on the starboard tack. Built in Boston in 1871, her tonnage of 952 was considered small by American standards.* (Author).

in a ship such as the *Henry B. Hyde* of 2,463 tons which was built at Bath, Maine, in 1884 by Chapman & Flint.

Of the ships built immediately after the Civil War, *Seminole* and *Pactolus* of 1,438 and 1,204 tons respectively were good examples of the new type of medium clipper which could carry a large cargo and yet have a fair turn of speed. The former was built at Mystic in 1865 with dimensions of 196.0 ft × 41.6 ft × 25.0 ft and cost $125,000. She made twenty-one passages outward to San Francisco from New York averaging 126 days, the fastest being her maiden passage which only took 96 days, 3 December 1865 to 9 February 1866. This is fully up to clipper ship standards.

In 1868, Donald McKay launched a full-bodied ship called *Sovereign of the Seas* and by no means the full-blood of fifteen years earlier. This new ship was built for the California trade around Cape Horn and measured 1,443 tons, but her shortest passage to San Francisco occupied 138 days.

However, in the following year, McKay built an improved version of a medium clipper, namely the *Glory of the Seas*. She measured 240.2 ft × 44.1 ft × 28.0 ft and 2,009 tons, and could carry from 3,300 to 3,600 tons. She had three decks, a big sheer and crossed a skysail on the mainmast only. The timber comprising her framework was of large size and occupied much valuable space in the hold, but that was the price to pay for a wooden ship. Although McKay built her on speculation, he spared no expense to make her a handsome vessel and gave her a figurehead of a Greek goddess mounted on an old-fashioned head and supported by carved trailboards.

No purchaser had been found for the ship, so McKay sailed aboard her for the maiden passage, instructing his captain to drive her and make a fast passage, but this

The magnificent Glory of the Seas *was the last sailing ship built by Donald McKay. Seen here at San Francisco in about 1877, the 'built-up' lower masts with their prominent metal hoops were a distinctive feature.* (San Francisco Maritime Museum).

was not to be. She took 120 days to San Francisco, and the day after her arrival, Donald McKay had the mortification to learn that his *Glory of the Seas* had been sold in order to satisfy his creditors. He owed a quarter of a million dollars and was now a ruined man. Under a new captain, the medium clipper was chartered to load grain at £3 5s (£3.25) per ton for Queenstown for orders. Back in Boston, McKay's shipyard and machinery was sold and his debts were met, but he never built another square-rigger. *Glory of the Seas* proved a fitting memorial to this clipper ship genius. Her fastest passage to San Francisco was one of 96 days from New York, made in 1873–74. After a long career she was finally burnt for her metal in 1923.

Another fine medium clipper built in 1869 was the *Great Admiral*, and she too possessed a fine figurehead, when the majority of ships were being given only billet heads. She was constructed at the yard of Robert E. Jackson, East Boston, and registered 1,497 tons, being built for W. F. Weld & Co of Boston whose flag she flew for 28 years. She was carefully and strongly built, and was always much admired both for her looks and for her speed. Amongst her fastest passages may be cited the following: Hong Kong to New York, 95 days in 1884; New York to Melbourne, 73 days in 1887; New York to San Francisco, 111 days in 1879.

The Suez Canal did not have the same impact on the Down-Easters as it did on the British tea clippers, and the former continued to slide down the ways in ever increasing numbers. The crews for these ships were supplied by crimps from the seamen's boarding houses, and hell-ships such as the *St Paul* had difficulty in procuring a crew.

Completing her fitting-out at Bath, Maine, the newly-launched ship St. Paul *was a fine specimen of naval architecture. The scene is at Chapman's shipyard in 1874 and the figures on her deck indicate her size: 1894 tons and a length of 228.2 ft.* (San Francisco Maritime Museum).

On one occasion the number could only be made up in San Francisco by shanghai-ing anyone that could be found, and an innocent Baptist minister came-to aboard the ship and outward-bound for Liverpool around Cape Horn. It was useless to remonstrate and he was soon adept at going aloft. Friends sent his passage money to Liverpool so that he could return home as a fare-paying passenger by a safer route.

Two fast ships were built at Boston for the ownership of H. Hastins: the *North American* of 1873 and the *South American* of 1875. In 1894, the latter took only 88 days between Cardiff and Hong Kong, laden with coal.

In Canada, the building of large wooden ships for sale to Liverpool shipowners continued throughout the sixties, although after 1870 British owners preferred their own iron or steel-hulled ships. When building for sale abroad, the sailing qualities were important and some of the ships built in the sixties must have been of clipper stock, such as the *Great Australia* of 1,661 tons which was built at St John in 1860 for Wright's of Liverpool; or the *Queen of Beauty* of 1,235 tons which was constructed at St John in 1861 for Fernie Bros of Liverpool. Another fast ship was the *Sunda* of 1,556 tons, built on the Miramichi in 1865 and owned by the Black Ball Line. In their old age, these strained and water-soaked ships were reduced to carrying guano from Chile or timber from Canada, and many were destroyed by fire.

Some fine medium clippers of smaller size were built in America such as the barque *Albemarle*, a model of which is in the Smithsonian Institution. She was launched in 1878 at Baltimore and measured 566 tons. From lines taken off the half-model by

The barque Tidal Wave *photographed in her later years, clewing up her sails. She was built in 1869 at Port Madison, Washington, by Bryant of 603 tons. Many American ships had a leg-of-mutton spanker such as the one she is setting.* (San Francisco Maritime Museum).

Howard I. Chapelle it can be seen that she had little deadrise but sharp ends and a big sheer. She was one of the fastest vessels engaged in the coffee trade from Rio de Janeiro. Other craft in this trade carried the rigs of brig and brigantine.

On the West Coast of America, it was customary to build vessels that were good sailers and to provide them with a big sail area, and the barquentine rig became popular after 1870. Howard Chapelle gives the lines and sail plan of one, the *W. H. Diamond*, as Figure 58 in *History of American Sailing Ships*. She was flat-floored with a sharp hollow entrance but a fuller run. Of 390 tons, whe was built in 1881.

It is stretching the definition of a 'clipper' to start including fine-lined or semi-fine-lined ships built here and there after the seventies, when the conditions which governed the building and operating of clippers had ceased to exist. The later medium clippers are included as a mark of courtesy to the origins from which they stemmed, because they and the full-bodied carriers which succeeded them are worthy of a study on their own.

[Left] *This is a good example of a doctored photograph, as the picture of the* Benjamin F. Packard, *built in 1883, was altered to supposedly represent the* Golden Sea, *built in 1864. The double topsails on the original have been converted into single ones, and the fore skysail has had the yard hoisted further up and now looks too deep a sail. Stunsail booms have been added under several of the yards, and the reef points are drawn as thick as the fore stay!* (National Maritime Museum).

[Right] *The ship* Santa Clara *in dry dock. She was built at Bath, Maine, in 1876 and was of 1535 tons. There is doubling skin of planking at the waterline level laid on top of the original planks and at a different angle to them.* (San Francisco Maritime Museum).

[**Left**] *The ship* Panay *sailing from Boston in about 1898, bound for Manila. She was built in 1877 at Boston and was of 1190 tons.* (Peabody Museum of Salem).

[**Right**] *The decks of the* Three Brothers, *looking aft from the foc'sle. She was built in 1856–7 as the ps* Vanderbilt *for the financier of that name, and was converted to a three-masted ship in 1873, with a tonnage of 2963 net. The main yard was 100 ft long.* (San Francisco Maritime Museum).

CHAPTER TEN

Later British Clippers

The races and exploits of the iron clippers and medium clippers built in the 1870s are almost better known than those of their composite sisters of the previous decade, partly because many of the captains, officers and seamen who manned them were still hale and hearty when Basil Lubbock and other writers took up their pens in the first decade of the present century to record their stories, and partly because many ships survived until recent times. The opening of the Suez Canal in 1869 completely altered the China tea trade and gave steamers preference over the clippers both in the matter of freight rates and in despatch. There was keen racing between the steamers, and the 10s per ton premium for the first ship home with new teas was re-introduced in their favour. Clippers now usually could not complete their loading until some time in July, and many sailed with the favourable monsoon. Others took cargoes to New York. But the Australian trade was still relatively free from steam competition as bunkering depots were widely spaced and sailing ships could carry cargo more cheaply on this long haul.

The opening of the Suez Canal temporarily curtailed clipper ship building for a year or two as owners of sailing ships waited to see the outcome, but three tea clippers were launched in 1870. Two of them were sister ships, the *Hallowe'en* and the unlucky *Blackadder*, and were both built on the Thames at Greenwich by Maudslay, Sons & Field for John Willis, owner of the *Cutty Sark*. The builders were not experienced in constructing sailing ships with the result that there were faults in the mast fittings and rigging, and *Blackadder* was dismasted on her maiden passage. The ensuing lawsuits between Willis, the underwriters and the builders resulted in the *Hallowe'en*, which was launched in June 1870, not being handed over to the owner until late the next year.

These two clippers were built of iron and were fast in light winds; their coefficient of under deck tonnage, .55, made them as sharp as *Cutty Sark*. The *Hallowe'en* registered 920 tons with dimensions of 216.6 ft × 35.2 ft × 20.5 ft. Her biggest day's run was 360 miles in the Roaring Forties. Although too late to load tea in 1872, she made a very fast maiden passage to Sydney of only 69 days, 1 July to 8 September 1872. In the China trade she had a remarkable average because her first three homeward passages between Shanghai or Woosung and London averaged $91\frac{2}{3}$ days. Even though she sailed late in the season during the favourable monsoon, this is a most unusual record. She was finally wrecked in 1887 off Salcombe with a cargo of tea from Foochow.

The third tea clipper to be built in 1870, the *Lothair*, also came from a yard on the Thames, being constructed by William Walker at Rotherhithe of 794 tons. Walker was also her first owner until Killick, Martin & Co purchased her in 1873. On her first passage from China under their house flag, commanded by Benjamin Orchard, she took her departure from Hong Kong on 11th December 1873 and passed the Scillies only 84 days out, but unfortunately took a further five days to reach Deal. In 1878 she made another swift tea-laden passage; on this occasion she was only 84 days between Amoy and New York. In 1873, she had loaded tea at £3 per ton, but at Hong Kong in October 1883 she could only get the miserably low freight of £1.37½ per ton for general cargo to New York. Extreme clippers could not be operated on such low rates, and many shipowners were disposing of their clippers in the eighties.

In his book, *By Way of Cape Horn*, Paul Stevenson records a story about her, as told by the captain:

'We were running our easting down...when we sighted a vessel astern. It was blowing hard from the nor'west, and the next time I looked, a couple of hours later, there was the ship close on our quarter, and we doing 12 knots. "Holy jiggers", says I to the mate, "there's the 'Flying Dutchman'." "Naw", says he, "it's the *Thermopylae*." But when she was abeam a little later, she hoisted her name, the *Lothair*, and its been my opinion ever since that she was making mighty close to 17 knots.'

Lothair survived until about 1910.

At Aberdeen in 1870, Alexander Hall had launched the composite ship *Lufra*, and Walter Hood had produced the wooden-hulled *Aviemore* of 1,091 tons for George Thompson & Co. As Thompson had had several successful composite ships and the iron *Patriarch*, it seems an anachronism for him to have ordered a wooden ship; certainly, all his subsequent vessels were built of iron.

The Australian trade now beckoned sailing ships and many an outward passage was made there, the ship then clearing either direct for home or else for San Francisco to load grain for Europe, for Calcutta to load jute for New York or Europe, or for an Eastern or Chinese port. These were routes which did not fit in with steamer schedules until boilers and engines became more efficient later in the century and coal consumption could be reduced.

Six fast ships in the 1,200 tons range had been built in the years 1869–70 for the 'Loch Line', of which the *Loch Ness* was possibly the fastest, having a passage of 67 days to Melbourne to her credit, made in 1874–75. In 1871, Hood & Co at Aberdeen launched the *Miltiades*, and the following year came the *Mermerus* from Barclay, Curle & Co's yard at Glasgow. She was built to the order of Carmichael of Greenock, all of whose ships were named after characters in the Golden Fleece legend. With a register tonnage of 1,671, she now set the pattern for the big clippers of the next few years. Plans of the ship appeared as Figures 271–3 in *Fast Sailing Ships*. Although her breadth and depth of hold had only increased by 3 ft 9 in and 2 ft 6 in respectively when compared with *Cutty Sark*, her length had shot up by 52 ft 0 in. This extra length gave her a higher speed potential. Her dimensions were now 264.2 ft × 39.8 ft × 23.7 ft. She had a small rise of floor but long sharp ends without much hollow in them; the forefoot was rounded and the stem swung up into a graceful bow with a fine figurehead and carved trail boards. There was a full height poop and forecastle with a large deckhouse between the fore and main masts. Aloft, she carried seven yards on each mast: above the courses, there were double topsails, double topgallants, royals and skysails, and stunsails in addition.

The above forms a typical description of the majority of the iron clippers built up to 1876 or so, although sometimes the skysails were omitted on fore and mizen masts. Many ships were painted black externally, but the fashion of 'painted ports' was increasing; these simulated gun ports necessitated a three-colour scheme of white,

[**Above**] *Lying on a mooring in the River Thames off Gravesend is the iron-hulled tea clipper* Hallowe'en, *built in 1870. A twin-funnelled paddle tug is at anchor in the foreground.* (Author).

[**Right**] *The fine-lined stern of the tea clipper* Lothair *taken during her last years when reduced to barque rig and owned in South America. It was wonderful how adaptable these beautifully-built ships were to almost any trade.* (The late Arthur D. Edwardes).

black and grey. The number of ports usually worked out to approximately one port for every hundred tons. Ships like *Mermerus* were capable of passages to Melbourne of less than 70 days and to Sydney of less than 75 days.

By 1873 some splendid iron clippers were being launched from shipyards in Scotland and the north of England, and of a larger size than iron vessels built before, but as the sail plans were augmented in proportion to the size of the hull, so there appeared many very heavily-rigged ships with yards of immense length. At first not all the shipbuilders were capable of manufacturing cheeks, trestle tress, fids or bobstays of sufficient strength to withstand the enormous strains which the tremendous weight of spars exerted on them. The great pressure of wind-maddened canvas was a force not properly calculated and serious dismastings took place on some ships. If the heel of a mast settled slightly or buckled under pressure, then the standing rigging slackened appreciably leaving the mast unsupported; the whole towering pyramid of sails and spars would then crumple with spars crashing down on deck, and blocks raining down on to the heads of the luckless crew. Masts were never cut away, because axes made no impression on an iron or steel mast; but the lanyards between the deadeyes could be cut through, and that would bring the masts down, possibly tearing up the deck, puncturing the hatches or gouging open the sides of the hull in the process. Under such circumstances it was amazing that anything could be saved from the wreckage to fashion a jury rig which could get the ship into port.

Most of the dismastings occurred in 1874 when the ships *Loch Ard, John Kerr, Cambridgeshire, Rydal Hall, Norval, Chrysomene* and *British Admiral* arrived in pu.· under jury rig. *Loch Ard* was actually dismasted twice, but the first time she put back to the Clyde to be refitted. The previous year, *Dallam Tower* and *Loch Maree* had been dismasted bound to Melbourne.

Amongst the best known iron clippers built in 1873 can be singled out the *Hesperus* of 1,777 tons constructed by Robert Steele & Co at Greenock, who had given up building composite clippers; *Loch Maree* built by Barclay, Curle & Co; *Samuel Plimsoll* built by Hood at Aberdeen; *Glengarry* from Royden's yard at Liverpool for the Calcutta trade and known as the 'clipper of the Indian Ocean'; *British Ambassador* of 1,794 tons built by Potter & Hodgkinson at Liverpool; and *Thomasina McLellan* built by McMillan of Dumbarton. The *British Ambassador* was owned by the British Shipowners Co of Liverpool and all their ships began with the word 'British'. She cost £42,000 and was very heavily rigged with a main yard 108 ft long; she was also very sharp in the entrance and run, to judge by a photograph of her builder's half-model. Her maximum recorded speed was 17 knots.

The year 1874 produced another set of wonderful, fast and beautiful ships: *Lammermoor* from John Reid's yard on the Clyde crossing seven yards on each mast; *Rodney* built by Pile of Sunderland; *Thessalus* by Barclay, Curle & Co of Glasgow for the 'Golden Fleece line'; and *Timaru* built by Scott & Co of Greenock. A plan of the latter, drawn and published by Harold A. Underhill, shows a hull broadly similar to *Mermerus*, a trifle fuller in the ends but with more deadrise and easier bilges. Being smaller than the latter, with a tonnage of 1,306, *Timaru* and her sister *Oamaru* set single topgallants and a skysail on the mainmast only. The *Thessalus* was a fast ship, trading to Australia, India and California. On one occasion bound to Calcutta, she was carrying a pack of foxhounds for the Jackal Club when she encountered a cyclone. The hounds were let out of their kennel in case of disaster just before a big sea burst over the rail and swept the kennel overboard. After the cyclone had passed, the foxhounds came

[**Right**] *The lofty wool clipper*
Mermerus *lies at the wharf in Victoria
Dock, Melbourne, in 1896. Her stunsails have been lopped off, but she still
crosses a skysail yard on the mainmast; her jibboom has been hauled inboard to minimize the risk of damage.*
(C. L. Hume).

[**Below**] *Sail plan of the* Argonaut,
*built at Glasgow in 1876 by Barclay,
Curle & Co with a length of 241 ft and
a tonnage of 1488. On the mainmast
only there are double topgallants and a
skysail, thus making seven yards on
this mast but five each on the other
two.* (Author).

out from under the bunks in the foc'sle where they had been hiding.

It was common practice for animals to be shipped on the deck of a sailing ship. On another occasion, *Thessalus* took horses from Melbourne to Calcutta and returned with camels. When *Dallam Tower* was dismasted in a hurricane in 1873, the prize bulls she was carrying on deck were washed overboard, and another ship saw one swimming about. Unfortunately, it could not be recovered.

The last composite clipper ship ever built, the *Torrens*, was launched in 1875 from the Sunderland yard of James Laing. She was a popular ship with passengers and remained in the Adelaide trade in which she made some fast passages such as 65 days from Plymouth to Adelaide in 1880–81 and 67 days in 1887–88. In 1893, Joseph Conrad made a voyage on her as first mate under the command of Captain Cope, and Galsworthy was a passenger on the passage from Adelaide to Cape Town.

Of other ships built in 1875, there was the lovely *Cedric the Saxon* of 1,619 tons and 260 ft long; she was probably a sister to the *Lammermoor* and carried a large sail area with a main yard 108 ft long. The pillars at the break of her poop were carved with heads from characters in Walter Scott's 'Waverley' novels. She has been immortalized in a lovely painting by Jack Spurling. Another fast ship was the *Loch Garry* whose fastest outward passage to Melbourne was one of 71 days from the Tuskar Light at the mouth of the Clyde, to Cape Otway made in 1892. George Thompson ordered an extreme clipper from Hood for the China trade and this ship was the *Salamis*, launched

After partial dismasting at Mauritius, the Serapis *has rigged sheer legs above the mainmast in order to get the lower mast on end. Sailors were obliged to carry out such work if shipyard facilities were non-existent or to save unnecessary expense.* (Author).

in 1875 and said to have been built on *Thermopylae*'s lines, but 10 ft longer. In fact, she only made one passage loaded with China tea but proved to be a fast and successful ship in taking wool back to London. Another clipper, the *Serapis*, was built for the China trade in 1876, but her passages were slow and she could only load at low freight rates. She traded until 1912 when she was broken up in Genoa.

The first of about fifty four-masted full-rigged ships was launched in 1875, with the name of *County of Peebles*, but her sail area was less than the three-masted *Mermerus*, in spite of having a hull of roughly similar size. Fine-lined clipper ships were on the decline although magnificent ships were being sent down the ways each year, and many could notch up a record passage. Stunsails and other flying kites were being discarded, crews cut down, small full-rigged ships being converted into barques. Commercial sail had many years yet to run but the real clippers' days were over. The *Cutty Sark* alone has survived to remind us of their queenliness and mysterious beauty.

The Aberdeen-built iron clipper Aristides *came from Walter Hood's yard in 1876. She is here seen outward bound off Sydney Heads, having just dropped the pilot and cast off the tug.* (R. W. Glassford).

[Left] *Looking forward from lifeboat, with main rigging in foreground.* (C. L. Hume).

Scenes aboard Macquarie.

[Above] *Under reduced canvas in a fresh breeze, the* Macquarie *is making good speed. Built in 1875 as the* Melbourne, *she was renamed in 1888 when sold by R. & H. Green to Devitt & Moore.* (R. W. Glassford).

[Left] *In calm weather, the crew on the main yard shifting the mainsail and overhauling the gear.* (C. L. Hume).

APPENDIX

PRINCIPAL RECORD PASSAGES MADE BY CLIPPERS

These have been compiled by my own researches amongst contemporary newspapers, log-books and published works. Two lists of record passages which are most valuable are Carl C. Cutler's *Five Hundred Sailing Records of American Built Ships*, and the compilation by Basil Lubbock in *Lloyd's Calendar*.

With even a log-book to verify it, the calculation of passage times down to the nearest hour and minute calls for a degree of precision which the actual course of events do not always justify. Times from 'pilot to pilot' or from 'land to land' make good reading but the ship's actual position at any one time is not always specified. These passage times are calculated to the nearest whole day.

CHINA TO ENGLAND AGAINST SW MONSOON

Year	Ship	Arrival and departure	Days	Remarks
186?	*Titania*	Woosung to Deal	96	
1869	*Sir Lancelot*	Foochow to Lizard	85	(to Dungeness 87)
1869	*Thermopylae*	Foochow to Lizard	89	(to London 91)

CHINA TO ENGLAND WITH NE MONSOON

1863	*Zingra*	Shanghai to Liverpool	85	
1863–64	*Nonpareil*	Shanghai to Liverpool	87	
1858	*Lord of the Isles*	Shanghai to Lizard	88	(to Dover 89)
1855	*Nightingale*	Shanghai to Beachy Head	91	(left 16 Feb)
1874–75	*Hallowe'en*	Shanghai to Start Point	89	(to London 91)
1867–68	*Elizabeth Nicholson*	Foochow to London	92	
1864–65	*Taeping*	Amoy to Deal	88	
1861	*Scawfell*	Canton River to Liverpool	87	(from Whampoa 88)
1873–74	*Lothair*	Hong Kong to Scillies	83	(to Deal 88) (to London 89)
1852	*Witch of the Wave*	Canton to Dungeness	90	(to mouth of English Channel 86)

ENGLAND TO CHINA AGAINST NE MONSOON

1863–64	*Fiery Cross*	London to Shanghai	92	
1866–67	*Ariel*	Start Point to Hong Kong	82	(pilot to pilot 80)

ENGLAND TO CHINA WITH SW MONSOON

1854	*Comet*	Liverpool to Hong Kong	84	
1866	*Maitland*	Sunderland to Hong Kong	87	
1853	*Cairngorm*	Lisbon to Hong Kong	72	(time at sea from London 77)
1863	*Ocean Mail*	London to Shanghai	88	

CHINA TO AMERICA WITH NE MONSOON

1849	*Sea Witch*	Hong Kong to New York	$74\frac{1}{2}$
1847–48	*Sea Witch*	Canton to New York	77
1859–60	*Swordfish*	Shanghai to New York	81

AMERICA TO CHINA WITH SW MONSOON

| 1850 | *Oriental* | New York to Hong Kong | $80\frac{1}{2}$ |

AMERICA TO CHINA AGAINST NE MONSOON

| 1851–52 | *Samuel Russell* | New York to Canton | 93 |

TRANS-PACIFIC

1853	*Swordfish*	San Francisco to Shanghai	$32\frac{1}{2}$
1878	*Ringleader*	Shanghai to San Francisco	30
1852	*Challenge*	Hong Kong to San Francisco	33
1878	*Kaisow*	Shanghai to Victoria	34

ENGLAND TO AUSTRALIA

1868–69	*Thermopylae*	Lizard to Cape Otway	60	(London to Melbourne 63)
1854–55	*James Baines*	Liverpool to Melbourne	64	(land to land 58)
1874–75	*Ben Voirlich*	Plymouth to Melbourne	64	
1869–70	*Patriarch*	London to Sydney	74	(pilot to pilot 67)
1872	*Hallowe'en*	London to Sydney	69	
1853–54	*Lord of the Isles*	Greenock to Sydney	74	(to Cape Otway 66)

AMERICA TO AUSTRALIA

| 1855 | *Mandarin* | New York to Melbourne | 70 |

AUSTRALIA TO ENGLAND

| 1854 | *Lightning* | Melbourne to Liverpool | 63 | |
| 1869 | *Patriarch* | Sydney to Ushant | 68 | (to London 69) |

AMERICA (East Coast) TO CALIFORNIA

1859–60	*Andrew Jackson*	New York to San Francisco	$89\frac{1}{6}$
1854	*Flying Cloud*	New York to San Francisco	$89\frac{1}{3}$
1851	*Flying Cloud*	New York to San Francisco	$89\frac{7}{8}$

CALIFORNIA to EAST COAST OF AMERICA OR EUROPE

EUROPE TO CALIFORNIA

TRANSATLANTIC

Larger scale copies of the plans reproduced in this book can be obtained on application to the Author, as well as plans of other sailing ships.

Index